AQA REVISION

T0326065

GCSE 9–1
A CHRISTMAS CAROL
BY CHARLES DICKENS

GREAT ANSWERS

SCHOLASTIC

Published in the UK by Scholastic, 2020

Scholastic Distribution Centre, Bosworth Avenue, Tournament Fields, Warwick, CV34 6UQ

Scholastic Ireland, 89E Lagan Road, Dublin Industrial Estate, Glasnevin, Dublin, D11 HP5F

SCHOLASTIC and associated logos are trademarks and/or registered trademarks of Scholastic Inc.

© Scholastic, 2020

A CIP catalogue record for this book is available from the British Library.

ISBN 978-1407-18398-5

Printed and bound by Leo Paper Products, China

The FSC® label means that the materials used for thisproduct come from well-managed sources

3 4 5 6 7 8 9   4 5 6 7 8 9 0 1 2 3

Every effort has been made to trace copyright holders for the works reproduced in this book, and the Publishers apologise for any inadvertent omissions.

Authors
Cindy Torn

Editorial team
Audrey Stokes, Vicki Yates, Kate Pedlar, Julia Roberts

Typesetting
Jayne Rawlings/Oxford Raw Design

Design team
Dipa Mistry

Contents

About this book

This book is designed to demonstrate what a great answer for your AQA GCSE English Literature exam question on *A Christmas Carol* (Paper 1, Section B) looks like. It demonstrates a step-by-step process from first sight of the question through to a full answer. This process shows you how to approach each step, from analysing what the question is asking you to do, to planning your answer, showing how it meets the assessment objectives for the exam paper and finally presenting a great answer and an examiner's response. All the answers in this book have been written in the light of advice from examiners and using tips drawn from the examiners' reports over the last few years.

It is important to note that one question can give rise to multiple different great answers. What these great answers all have in common is that they are based on an excellent interpretation with sound exploration of **evidence**. Great answers are not *right* answers, they are rich and well-argued answers.

In this book you will find the following features that will help you understand how to achieve that all-important great answer in your exam.

Zoom in on the question

Starting with this extract, explore how Dickens presents the supernatural in *A Christmas Carol*.

Write about:

- how Dickens presents the supernatural in this extract
- how Dickens presents the supernatural in the novel as a whole.

First focus on the extract to 'anchor' the answer and to explore some details about Dickens' presentation of the supernatural. (AO1/AO2)

Concentrate on Dickens' ideas and how he chooses his words to present those ideas. (AO1/AO2)

Stay relevant to the question focus: how Scrooge both resists and learns from the supernatural. (AO1)

Start with the extract but clarify/ explain details here with references to other parts of the novel. (AO1/AO2)

Analysis of the question to help you focus on what the question is actually asking you.

AO1 Explore Dickens' presentation of Fred as the **foil** to Scrooge. How does Dickens present Fred's generosity? Examine Fred's attitudes to Christmas, love and marriage, in contrast to those of Scrooge.

AO2 Explore their different attitudes towards Christmas – including symbolism of warmth and cold. Discuss Fred's constant joy: it's not about the situation in which we find ourselves but the way in which we find joy and love where we can.

AO3 How does Dickens use Fred to convey his message that warmth and addressing social responsibility can be found at Christmas? Relate Fred's treatment of Bob Cratchit to Dickens' social message.

Ideas to help you cover the AOs for each question and matching colour-coded commentary within the answers to show you how these are achieved.

Scrooge abides by the views of Thomas Malthus, arguing that 'if they [the poor] would rather die...they had better do it, and decrease the surplus population'④. In stark contrast, the spirit's generosity in this extract, giving incense 'To a poor one most', represents the social message of the importance of charity, understanding and generosity towards the people who need it most. The impact of these values is evident through the contrast between the 'good humour' of the community in the extract and the misery of Scrooge shown through the simile 'solitary as an oyster' in Stave One⑤. Dickens shows how the spirit of Christmas can bring generosity to the community and joy to the individual.

Dickens further presents the spirit of Christmas through the characters which embody it – notably, Fred, who in his first line of dialogue, exclaims 'A merry Christmas, uncle!', thus setting out his view of Christmas from

④ AO1/AO3: 'conceptual' approach – question focus viewed from perspective of Dickens' purpose.

⑤ AO2 (structure): clear understanding of how development of action through the novel help Dickens to shape meaning and effect.

Paragraph	Content		Timing
1	Intro – use the question prep to establish focus of answer.		9.40
2	Women's role as home-maker, for example, Mrs Cratchit. Women are not expected to mature or learn, for example, Fan – contrast with Scrooge's opportunities.		9.43
3	Household roles: women as wives and mothers who support the men around them. Men as head of the household.	Refer back to extract and focus of the question throughout. Consider what Dickens might want the reader to think about roles of the women in the novel.	9.58
4	Women and their role in Scrooge's redemption: Belle and Fan.		10.06
5	Women's role in the novel to bring joy to men.		10.14
6	Conclusion – brief return to question. Are these lessons relevant today?		10.22

Essay plans and timings to help you plan more efficiently.

DO IT!

Now use what you have learned to answer the following AQA exam-style question.

Starting with this moment in the novel, explore how Dickens presents ideas about family and home life in *A Christmas Carol*.

Write about:

- how Dickens presents ideas about family and home life in this extract
- how Dickens presents ideas about family and home life in the novel as a whole.

[30 marks]

AQA exam-style questions using the *same* extract provided for the Great Answer analysis which precedes it.

Exam-style questions using previously unseen text extracts, allowing you to put into practice the skills you've learned and create a great answer by yourself.

Online answers

These are designed to guide you towards structuring a really 'great answer' and consolidate your understanding through thought and application (including an AO breakdown). Remember: it is important to write your own answers before checking online at **www.scholastic.co.uk/gcse**.

Advice for students

✓ **Know your text well.** This will help you to demonstrate your knowledge and understanding in the exam. Concentrate on knowing the text well rather than predicting questions.

✓ **Read the question carefully and answer the question.** Be sure you are answering the question you have chosen and *not* the one that you would have preferred to see on the paper.

✓ **Take time to think about and plan your answer.** Gathering your thoughts will give you space to address the question and choose appropriate references and details to support and develop your answer.

✓ **Demonstrate your knowledge by referencing parts of the play.** But make sure it is relevant, you don't get extra marks for more quotations, but you do get more marks for making interesting comments about the references you have selected.

✓ **Read the extracts very carefully.** It is helpful to place the extract in the **context** of the play – at what point, what happened before and/or after, which characters are involved, how does it link to other parts of the text. Be sure that you understand the meaning and context of quotations you choose from the extract.

✓ **Recognise that 'writer's methods' means anything the writer has done deliberately.** This covers the writer's use of language and techniques, the **structure** of the text and characterisation.

✓ **Understand the connection between the writer's methods and the writer's ideas.** It might be helpful to think about *how* the writer does something and *why* the writer does something.

✓ **Link comments on contextual factors/ideas to the text.** Keep in mind that context informs but should never dominate your reading of the text; the text comes first. Relating the extract to the whole text is a valid approach to context.

Question 1

Read the following extract from Stave Three of *A Christmas Carol* and then answer the question that follows.

In this extract, Scrooge is with the Ghost of Christmas Present. He is watching a scene from Fred's Christmas party.

Scrooge's nephew revelled in another laugh, and, as it was impossible to keep the infection off, though the plump sister tried hard to do it with aromatic vinegar, his example was unanimously followed.

"I was only going to say," said Scrooge's nephew, "that the consequence of his taking a dislike to us, and not making merry with us, is, as I think, that he loses some pleasant moments, which could do him no harm. I am sure he loses pleasanter companions than he can find in his own thoughts, either in his mouldy old office or his dusty chambers. I mean to give him the same chance every year, whether he likes it or not, for I pity him. He may rail at Christmas till he dies, but he can't help thinking better of it – I defy him – if he finds me going there in good temper, year after year, and saying, 'Uncle Scrooge, how are you?' If it only puts him in the vein to leave his poor clerk fifty pounds, *that's* something; and I think I shook him yesterday."

It was their turn to laugh, now, at the notion of his shaking Scrooge. But, being thoroughly good-natured, and not much caring what they laughed at, so that they laughed at any rate, he encouraged them in their merriment, and passed the bottle, joyously.

After tea they had some music. For they were a musical family, and knew what they were about when they sung a Glee or Catch, I can assure you: especially Topper, who could growl away in the bass like a good one, and never swell the large veins in his forehead, or get red in the face over it. Scrooge's niece played well upon the harp; and played, among other tunes, a simple little air (a mere nothing: you might learn to whistle it in two minutes), which had been familiar to the child who fetched Scrooge from the boarding-school, as he had been reminded by the Ghost of Christmas Past.

Starting with this extract, explore how Dickens presents the character of Fred, Scrooge's nephew, in *A Christmas Carol*.

Write about:

- how Dickens presents Fred in this extract

- how Dickens presents Fred in the novel as a whole.

[30 marks]

Zoom in on the question

Starting with this extract, explore how Dickens presents the character of Fred, Scrooge's nephew, in *A Christmas Carol*.

Write about:

- how Dickens presents Fred in this extract
- how Dickens presents Fred in the novel as a whole.

Concentrate on Dickens' ideas about Fred and how he chooses his words to present those ideas, for example warm images. (AO2)

First focus on the extract to 'anchor' the answer and to explore details about Dickens' presentation of Fred. (AO1/AO2)

Stay relevant to the question focus to address AO1: how does Dickens present Fred?

Start with the extract but clarify/explain details here with references to other parts of the novel. (AO1/AO2)

Here are some ideas that could be included in an answer in order to cover the Assessment Objectives (AOs).

AO1 Explore Dickens' presentation of Fred as the **foil** to Scrooge. How does Dickens present Fred's generosity? Examine Fred's attitudes to Christmas, love and marriage, in contrast to those of Scrooge.

AO2 Explore their different attitudes towards Christmas – including symbolism of warmth and cold. Discuss Fred's constant joy: it's not about the situation in which we find ourselves but the way in which we find joy and love where we can.

AO3 How does Dickens use Fred to convey his message that warmth and addressing social responsibility can be found at Christmas? Relate Fred's treatment of Bob Cratchit to Dickens' social message.

A student has decided to focus on Fred as a foil to Scrooge. This is the plan they have made to answer the question.

Paragraph	Content		Timing
1	Intro – use the question prep to establish focus of answer.		9.40
2	Goodwill at Christmas – contrast between Fred and Scrooge. Symbolism of language of heat. Christmas valued by Fred; brings people together. Fred as a reminder of meaning of Christmas.		9.43
3	Fred as the foil to Scrooge – constant source of joy, even in the darkest situations. **Structure** – finding joy and love in what we can. Poverty in Victorian England and Dickens' social/moral message.	Refer back to extract and focus of the question throughout. Consider what Dickens might want the reader to think about Fred's role in the novel.	9.58
4	Love and generosity. Fred's attitude to marriage in comparison to that of Scrooge; Scrooge loses out from his lack of warmth. Fred's attitude towards love and how he aims to change Scrooge. Dickens' social message.		10.06
5	The love/generosity behind Fred's actions, with no expectation of reward. How Dickens presents Fred's generosity towards Bob Cratchit. How Dickens uses Fred to convey his message: the importance of warmth and meeting our social responsibilities.		10.14
6	Conclusion – brief return to question. Are these lessons relevant today?		10.22

The essay plan above will meet these Assessment Objectives:

AO1 Read, understand and respond	Explore the extract and the **evidence** of different attitudes towards Christmas: how Dickens presents Fred's generosity towards Bob Cratchit. Compare this with Scrooge and Fred in **Stave** Five.
AO2 Language, form and structure	Discuss Dickens' presentation of Fred as a contrast to Scrooge, for example through the symbolism of the language of heat. Examine Fred's attitudes to Christmas, love and marriage, in contrast to Scrooge's attitudes – through their language.
AO3 Contexts	Consider how Dickens uses Fred to convey his message: the warmth and fulfilling of social responsibility seen in goodwill at Christmastime. Analyse the extract in the **context** of the whole novel.

In this extract from Stave Three of *A Christmas Carol*, Fred is presented as kind and selfless[1]. The focus on Fred's merry attitudes towards Christmas, love and generosity show Fred as the antithesis to Scrooge; Dickens uses him as a means of conveying his social message of the importance of goodwill, in what may be regarded as an allegorical novel.

Fred is presented as regarding Christmas as a time of warmth, kindness and love. This love of Christmas is evident from the start of the extract, as the guests are unable to avoid the 'infection' of Fred's laughter[2]. This infectious laughter further reveals Scrooge's lack of humanity as he remains unmoved by Fred's merriment. Similarly, Scrooge's 'very small fire' in Stave One directly contrasts with the guests in Stave Three being 'clustered round the fire, by lamplight'. This description shows the contrast between Fred's love of community and Scrooge's stark solitude[3].

With his constant joy, shown through the references to him doing this with 'merriment' and 'joyously', Fred is presented as a foil to Scrooge[4]. This merriment is evident from Fred's entrance, in Stave One, where he 'cried in a cheerful voice'. Fred's joy continues into this extract, as 'Scrooge's nephew revelled in another laugh'. The reference to their familial relationship conveys the stark contrast between their attitudes and dispositions. The **verb** 'revelled' suggests Fred's sheer joy in the company of others, providing a striking contrast to Scrooge. Despite their differences, Fred is determined to include Scrooge, as his warmth towards Scrooge is maintained from his wishes of 'A merry Christmas, uncle!' in Stave One to the 'mercy he didn't shake his arm off' in welcome in Stave Five[5]. Fred maintains his good humour despite Scrooge's insulting remarks that he's 'poor enough'. Through Fred's constant joy, Dickens presents his moral message that generosity and kindness bring joy to all in spite of the inequalities and hardships of Victorian England.

Fred's love and generosity are further shown through his attitudes towards marriage and selflessness. In Stave One, Fred states that he married 'Because I fell in love'. This largely **monosyllabic** line conveys the importance of love above all else – an obvious truth to Fred[6]. Scrooge's mocking repetition of this statement about love, however, shows his disagreement, suggesting he views Fred's values as frivolous and unnecessary. Despite this disagreement about love, in this extract Dickens clearly reveals his message through Fred's values, as Fred states: 'I am sure he loses pleasanter companions than he can find in his own thoughts'. Fred's observation builds on the **narrator's** description of Scrooge in Stave One through the **simile** 'solitary as an oyster'. The image suggests Scrooge is closed off from society[7], implying that happiness can only be found through the loving values shown by Fred. Indeed, after Scrooge's redemption in Stave Five, he shows care towards his 'niece by marriage'; Dickens' subtle description that their relation comes from 'marriage' shows that Scrooge's heart has finally softened towards the concept of marriage, and family, because of Fred's actions.

Fred's attitude towards love is demonstrated by his everyday goodwill, evident in Stave One as he stops to bestow 'the greetings of the season on the clerk' – the verb 'bestow' showing Fred's sense of fellowship and goodwill. This love for those around him continues into the extract here: Fred views his determination to visit Scrooge every year as being worthwhile 'If it only puts him in the vein to leave his poor clerk fifty pounds'. This sentiment is in direct contrast to Scrooge's nature in Stave One[8]. The love and generosity behind Fred's actions disregarding any monetary gain, here and in the novel as a whole, perfectly conveys Dickens' social message: we should be driven by love, and will be happier for it[9].

Overall, Fred's goodwill and love are constant, both within the extract and throughout the novel[10]. The reader sees these traits as attractive and understandable, and Dickens provides Fred as a model to show us how to behave. Because of these positive traits, it is evident that Fred acts as a foil to Scrooge. Through this presentation of Fred, a character the reader admires and values, Dickens is able to successfully convey his message of the importance of selflessness and morality.

[8] AO3: useful comparison of use of **techniques** in the extract and in the novel as a whole.

[9] AO3: importance of social message of love and goodwill towards all.

[10] AO1/AO3: 'conceptual' approach – question focus viewed from the importance of social message.

Commentary
This is a critical and thoughtful response that develops a relevant and thorough answer to the question. It is a conceptualised answer based on subtle insights into aspects of goodwill and how Dickens presents Fred. Some profound insights are based on a fine appreciation of language details and how Dickens structures our responses to Fred through the novel.

DO IT!

Now use what you have learned to answer the following AQA exam-style question. Refer to the extract from Stave Three on page 6.

Starting with this extract, explore how Dickens presents ideas about happiness in *A Christmas Carol*.

Write about:

- how Dickens presents ideas about happiness in this extract

- how Dickens presents ideas about happiness in the novel as a whole.

[30 marks]

Question 2

Read the following extract from Stave One of *A Christmas Carol* and then answer the question that follows.

In this extract, it is Christmas Eve and Scrooge is closing the counting house. Scrooge is talking to the clerk, Bob Cratchit.

> Foggier yet, and colder! Piercing, searching, biting cold. If the good Saint Dunstan had but nipped the Evil Spirit's nose with a touch of such weather as that, instead of using his familiar weapons, then indeed he would have roared to lusty purpose. The owner of one scant young nose, gnawed and mumbled by the hungry cold as bones are gnawed by dogs, stooped down at Scrooge's keyhole to regale him with a Christmas carol: but at the first sound of –
>
> *"God bless you, merry gentleman!*
> *May nothing you dismay!"*
>
> Scrooge seized the ruler with such energy of action, that the singer fled in terror, leaving the keyhole to the fog and even more congenial frost.
>
> At length the hour of shutting up the counting-house arrived. With an ill will Scrooge dismounted from his stool, and tacitly admitted the fact to the expectant clerk in the tank, who instantly snuffed his candle out, and put on his hat.
>
> "You'll want all day tomorrow, I suppose?" said Scrooge.
>
> "If quite convenient, sir."
>
> "It's not convenient," said Scrooge, "and it's not fair. If I was to stop half a crown for it, you'd think yourself ill-used, I'll be bound?"
>
> The clerk smiled faintly.
>
> "And yet," said Scrooge, "you don't think *me* ill-used when I pay a day's wages for no work."
>
> The clerk observed that it was only once a year.
>
> "A poor excuse for picking a man's pocket every twenty-fifth of December!" said Scrooge, buttoning his great-coat to the chin. "But I suppose you must have the whole day. Be here all the earlier next morning."
>
> The clerk promised that he would; and Scrooge walked out with a growl. The office was closed in a twinkling, and the clerk, with the long ends of his white comforter dangling below his waist (for he boasted no great-coat), went down a slide on Cornhill, at the end of a lane of boys, twenty times, in honour of its being Christmas Eve, and then ran home to Camden Town as hard as he could pelt, to play at blind-man's buff.

Starting with this extract, explore how Dickens presents the world of work in *A Christmas Carol*.

Write about:

- how Dickens presents the world of work in this extract

- how Dickens presents the world of work in the novel as a whole.

[30 marks]

Zoom in on the question

> Starting with this extract, explore how Dickens presents the world of work in *A Christmas Carol*.
>
> Write about:
>
> - how Dickens presents the world of work in this extract
>
> - how Dickens presents the world of work in the novel as a whole.

First focus on the extract to 'anchor' the answer and to explore details of Scrooge as an employer. (AO1/AO2)

Concentrate on Dickens' ideas about the workplace and how he chooses his words to present those ideas. (AO2)

Start with the extract but clarify/explain details here with references to other parts of the novel. (AO1/AO2)

Stay relevant to the question focus – how Dickens presents the world of work – for example, through language showing the contrasts between Scrooge/Fezziwig/Fred. (AO1/AO2)

Here are some ideas that could be included in an answer in order to cover the Assessment Objectives (AOs).

AO1 Contrast different attitudes towards the world of work, including Scrooge's attitude, the happiness Fezziwig brings to his workers, Fred's generosity, and how Scrooge changes.

AO2 Discuss Scrooge's power over Bob Cratchit – shown through language, eg Scrooge's use of rhetorical questions to bully; contrast the 'expectant' clerk with Scrooge's bad-tempered responses. Discuss how Scrooge's attitudes are shown from Stave One: consider language subtleties, his treatment of Fred and his understanding of the poverty of the Cratchit family.

AO3 Show how Dickens uses Scrooge's attitudes to the world of work to convey his social message about employer responsibility. What does Dickens suggest is the impact of employers ignoring their social responsibilities?

A student has decided to focus on the gulf between the wealthy people and the poor working classes. This is the plan they have made to answer the question.

Paragraph	Content		Timing
1	Intro – use the question prep to establish focus of answer. Overarching idea: Dickens shows gulf between the wealthy employers and the poor working class.		9.40
2	Explore extract – evidence of different attitudes towards the world of work. Scrooge's power over Bob Cratchit – shown through language: Scrooge's use of rhetorical questions to bully; contrast the clerk and Scrooge.		9.43
3	How Scrooge's attitudes towards the world of work are shown from Stave One: language subtleties; his treatment of Fred; Fred's understanding of the poverty of the Cratchit family.	Refer back to extract and focus of the question throughout. Consider what Dickens might want the reader to think about the world of work.	9.58
4	How Dickens presents the positive side of the world of work: the happiness Fezziwig brings to his workers; Fred's generosity; how Scrooge changes at the end.		10.06
5	How Dickens uses Scrooge's attitudes to the world of work to convey his social message: the employer's responsibility; the effect on the poor if this is neglected.		10.14
6	Conclusion – brief return to question. Are these lessons relevant today?		10.22

The essay plan on the previous page will meet these Assessment Objectives:

AO1 Read, understand and respond	Explore how Dickens shows the gulf between the wealthy employers, for example, Scrooge and the poor working classes. Discuss attitudes towards the world of work: Scrooge and Bob Cratchit.
AO2 Language, form and structure	Consider Scrooge's power over Bob Cratchit – shown through language – and the contrasting, sensual, language used to describe Fezziwig.
AO3 Contexts	Discuss Dickens' use of Scrooge's attitudes towards the world of work to convey his message about employer responsibility.

11

Dickens' presentation of the world of work clearly emphasises the gulf between employer and employees in *A Christmas Carol*❶.

In the extract, Dickens presents contrasting attitudes towards the world of work through Scrooge and Cratchit. Dickens uses these two characters to represent the differing views of the employer and the employee. In the extract, we see how Scrooge uses rhetorical questions to test and bully Cratchit, emphasising their difference in status❷. When Scrooge grumbles, 'If I was to stop half a crown for it, you'd think yourself ill-used', he shows his lack of empathy for his clerk. These questions allow Scrooge to make accusations without giving Cratchit legitimate excuse to object to them. This bullying attitude is further illustrated by comments regarding paying 'a day's wages for no work', even though Dickens makes it clear that Cratchit is a hard worker❸. Describing Cratchit as the 'expectant clerk' suggests that Cratchit sees this behaviour as normal, further illustrating the gulf between the wealthy and poor.

Dickens reveals that Scrooge's attitude towards the world of work is not universally held when Fred enters in 'cheerful voice...[and]...all in a glow': allusions to heat here in stark contrast to the cold and 'frosty' images used to describe Scrooge earlier in Stave One. As Fred is Scrooge's social equal, Dickens is suggesting that being from the employing class does not necessitate meanness❹. Scrooge immediately attacks Fred's Christmas spirit and asks, 'What reason have you to be merry? You're poor enough', the contemptuous question revealing his belief that only wealth brings happiness. Dickens uses Fred's response to reiterate his social message, as Fred points out that although his uncle is rich he is not happy. Dickens later provides hope for the future workplace, in Stave Four, when Bob Cratchit reveals Fred's 'extraordinary kindness' towards him❺. Fred warmly expresses his condolences towards the Cratchit family, allowing Dickens to suggest the gulf between employer and employee may change.

In Stave Two, Dickens presents the positive side of the world of work through Fezziwig, Scrooge's first employer. Scrooge's joy at seeing him is shown through the exclamation, 'Bless his heart: it's Fezziwig alive again!' Dickens' use of soft consonants in the character name, 'f', 'zz' and 'w', suggests his warm personality❻, reiterated through his laughter and 'jovial voice'. Through the Ghost's comments about the cost of the Fezziwigs' 'domestic ball', as only being 'but a few pounds', Scrooge is shown that his money and kindness are paid back a thousand-fold in positivity from his workforce❼.

❶ **AO1:** clear opening, using words from the question to ensure relevance.

❷ **AO1:** critically explores the novel in relation to the question.

❸ **AO1:** precise choice of details to support points.

❹ **AO2:** insight into Dickens' craft as a writer.

❺ **AO2 (structure):** clear understanding of how development of action through the novel helps Dickens to shape meaning and effect.

❻ **AO2:** insight into how meaning is implied by language choices.

❼ **AO1:** precise choice of details to support points.

Scrooge makes it clear that he does as much as he thinks necessary to support the poor by his contributions to the 'Union workhouses', whilst in the same moment shows his contempt for the circumstances of those unfortunate enough to need them. Confusing destitution with idleness, we find Scrooge lamenting that he 'can't afford to make idle people merry'. Yet we know that he could certainly help some if he wished: he just doesn't think he should[8]. Indeed, Dickens presents Scrooge quoting a popular opinion of the wealthy classes: 'If they [the poor] would rather die... [rather than go into the workhouses]...they had better do it, and decrease the surplus population'. This lack of compassion voiced by a character presented as an employer allows Dickens to highlight the need for social change, and that wealthy employers are in a position to enact some of this reform[9]. Indeed, at the end of the novel, it is Scrooge's benevolence that saves Tiny Tim from death.

Dickens shows that as an employer it is not 'enough for a man to understand his own business', as this attitude will not bring wealth to society[10]. Dickens shows, through Fezziwig and Fred's actions towards workers and the workplace, that social responsibility will help workers and employers alike: a message reiterated by Tiny Tim's final blessing[11].

[8] **AO1**: quotation explained well.

[9] AO3: links to context.

[10] AO3: importance of social message of responsibility towards the workplace.

[11] **AO1**/AO3: 'conceptual' approach – question focus viewed from the importance of social message.

Commentary
This answer is based on a perceptive enquiry into Dickens' presentation of the world of work and the gulf between employers and their workers. It explores this difference and how it is revealed by Dickens' techniques that include contrasting characterisation (Fred, Fezziwig, Scrooge) and language choices. The analysis is well-structured and supported by well-chosen references that range widely across the text. Contextual knowledge informs the analysis rather than being separate.

DO IT!

Now use what you have learned to answer the following AQA exam-style question. Refer to the extract on page 10.

Starting with this extract, explore how Dickens presents ideas about power in *A Christmas Carol*.

Write about:

• how Dickens presents ideas about power in this extract

• how Dickens presents ideas about power in the novel as a whole.

[30 marks]

Question 3

Read the following extract from Stave One of *A Christmas Carol* and then answer the question that follows.

At this point in the novel, Scrooge is visited by the ghost of his business associate, Jacob Marley.

> Scrooge fell upon his knees, and clasped his hands before his face.
>
> "Mercy!" he said. "Dreadful apparition, why do you trouble me?"
>
> "Man of the worldly mind!" replied the Ghost. "Do you believe in me or not?"
>
> "I do," said Scrooge. "I must. But why do spirits walk the earth, and why do they come to me?"
>
> "It is required of every man," the Ghost returned, "that the spirit within him should walk abroad among his fellow-men, and travel far and wide; and if that spirit goes not forth in life, it is condemned to do so after death. It is doomed to wander through the world – oh, woe is me! – and witness what it cannot share, but might have shared on earth, and turned to happiness!"
>
> Again the spectre raised a cry, and shook its chain and wrung its shadowy hands.
>
> "You are fettered," said Scrooge, trembling. "Tell me why?"
>
> "I wear the chain I forged in life," replied the Ghost. "I made it link by link, and yard by yard; I girded it on of my own free will, and of my own free will I wore it. Is its pattern strange to *you*?"
>
> Scrooge trembled more and more.
>
> "Or would you know," pursued the Ghost, "the weight and length of the strong coil you bear yourself? It was full as heavy and as long as this, seven Christmas Eves ago. You have laboured on it since. It is a ponderous chain!"
>
> Scrooge glanced about him on the floor, in the expectation of finding himself surrounded by some fifty or sixty fathoms of iron cable, but he could see nothing.
>
> "Jacob," he said, imploringly. "Old Jacob Marley, tell me more! Speak comfort to me, Jacob!"
>
> "I have none to give," the Ghost replied.

Starting with this extract, explore how Dickens presents the supernatural in *A Christmas Carol*.

Write about:

- how Dickens presents the supernatural in this extract
- how Dickens presents the supernatural in the novel as a whole.

[30 marks]

Zoom in on the question

Starting with this extract, explore how Dickens presents the supernatural in *A Christmas Carol*.

Write about:

- how Dickens presents the supernatural in this extract
- how Dickens presents the supernatural in the novel as a whole.

First focus on the extract to 'anchor' the answer and to explore some details about Dickens' presentation of the supernatural. (AO1/AO2)

Concentrate on Dickens' ideas and how he chooses his words to present those ideas. (AO1/AO2)

Stay relevant to the question focus: how Scrooge both resists and learns from the supernatural. (AO1)

Start with the extract but clarify/explain details here with references to other parts of the novel. (AO1/AO2)

Here are some ideas that could be included in an answer so as to cover the Assessment Objectives (AOs).

AO1 Is the reader meant to be afraid of the ghosts or are they symbols? Consider Jacob Marley: his role as a 'friend' to Scrooge as he issues the warning.

AO2 Note the strength of Scrooge's words (scornful). His attitude and behaviour change throughout the novel and so does the reader's reaction to him. Discuss Marley's message and how he is 'fettered' by chains he 'forged' himself. Refer to the symbolic representation of the chains as cash-boxes and ledgers. Consider the theatrical function and dramatic presentation of the ghosts.

AO3 Explore Dickens' message. Would a modern reader be more or less likely to accept that we need to take responsibility for each other in order to avoid 'Ignorance' and 'Want'? Discuss context of Christian teachings and endless purgatory.

A student has decided to focus on the role the ghosts play in Scrooge's redemption. This is the plan they have made to answer the question.

Paragraph	Content		Timing
1	Intro – use the question preparation to establish focus of answer. Is Dickens' intention to frighten or to instruct – or to frighten in order to instruct?		9.40
2	Evidence of Dickens' presentation of the supernatural. Jacob Marley and his role in establishing the supernatural as driver for the **plot** – pay attention to language subtleties.		9.43
3	How Dickens uses supernatural elements to lead Scrooge towards redemption – contemporary and modern beliefs.	Refer back to extract and focus of the question throughout. Consider what Dickens might want the reader to think about the supernatural.	9.58
4	Dickens' presentation of the three Christmas ghosts as a device to convey his social message.		10.06
5	Role of Ignorance and Want in the 'present' – both for Dickens and the modern reader – Dickens' social message.		10.14
6	Conclusion – brief return to question. Are these lessons relevant today?		10.22

The essay plan above will meet these Assessment Objectives:

AO1 Read, understand and respond	Explore the relationship between Scrooge and the supernatural, considering how Dickens might want the reader to react. Use evidence to support insights.
AO2 Language, form and structure	Explore what Dickens says about the ghosts and what they teach Scrooge. Consider his methods and his **viewpoint**. Refer ghosts as driver for the **plot's** structure – extract from the start of the novel.
AO3 Contexts	Discuss the relevance of contemporary and modern assumptions about the supernatural and social responsibility. Consider the location of extract in the context of whole novel.

In *A Christmas Carol*, Dickens presents each supernatural[1] 'Dreadful apparition' as forces to instruct Scrooge as they lead him towards his redemption.

In this extract from the start of the novel, Dickens presents Marley's ghost in the role of friend to Scrooge as he issues a warning. This warning delivers Dickens' social message[2]. He is 'fettered', bound by the chains he has forged through his actions, with the metallic images suggesting the strength of his guilt. The chains, which **symbolise** his life's main motivators (business and money), are made of 'cash-boxes, keys, padlocks' and will bind him[3]. Dickens refers to Marley's hands as 'shadowy', playing on associations of ghosts and darkness, causing the reader to doubt what is real and what is not in order to promote a sense of fear. Dickens presents the perpetual torture of wandering 'through the world' being forced to 'witness' hardship as Marley's punishment for not helping others during his lifetime, when he had the chance to act, rather than witness, and turn his suffering 'to happiness'. Scrooge has 'laboured' on his own chain, the verb suggesting unpleasant toil and hardship. However, Dickens presents this labour as Scrooge's own choice. He has pursued wealth rather than happiness. Dickens drives his point further when Marley is unable to offer comfort to Scrooge because he has 'none to give': the extent of Scrooge's peril is emphasised when Marley reminds him that he has continued to forge the 'strong coil' he bears for an additional 'seven years'[4].

Marley's message establishes the visitation of three further spirits, which provides the structure of the novel and Scrooge's path to redemption[5]. With Marley's warning that what preoccupies you in life will bind you in death, Dickens links Marley's fate to Christian depictions of purgatory, where there is 'No rest, no peace' – a familiar concept to a contemporary reader[6]. However, overall, the reader is probably more intrigued by the ghosts than terrified. Dickens presents the ghosts as symbols of Scrooge's redemption rather than evil figures. Even the most sinister, the Ghost of Christmas Yet to Come, has a 'kind hand'[7].

The three Christmas ghosts, together, are a device to explore Dickens' social message around the impact of poverty and everyone's responsibility in easing it. The Ghost of Christmas Past, an unsettling and 'strange' apparition shifting between childlike and aged impressions, reveals events and choices that have shaped Scrooge's life, forging the man he is in the present. The ghost represents our need to examine the events that make us[8]. The child and old man within one body show how the innocence of childhood remains within as we grow older. The Ghost of Christmas Present is described as 'jolly', representing the lack of regret and sorrow

1 AO1: clear opening, using words from the question to ensure relevance.

2 AO1/AO3: 'conceptual' approach – question focus viewed from **POV** of Dickens' purpose.

3 AO1: deft choices of details to support points.

4 AO3: Scrooge's plight here set in context of whole novel.

5 AO2: insight into structure of the novel and drivers of the plot.

6 AO1/AO3: subtle development of analysis of how Dickens presents the supernatural within a Christian context.

7 AO3: insight into how Dickens *develops* our understanding of the supernatural and how it changes.

8 AO1/AO2: an exploratory response and sensitivity to language and form is leading to deeper insights into Dickens' message.

in youth that may exist in old age. Scrooge realises that he can 'Profit' from the ghost's teaching, which is a move away from only regarding profit in monetary terms. However, within the Ghost of Christmas Present's robes lurk 'Ignorance' and 'Want', two children symbolising the ills of contemporary times.[9] Dickens refers to the Ghost of Christmas Yet to Come as a 'Phantom', suggesting darkness and death and links to the Grim Reaper. Dickens shows the reader the fate of those who care for money more than human relationships and social responsibility through his use of contrasts between light and dark and between happiness and deep sorrow[10].

The supernatural beings in the novel all present Dickens' message to society. The Ghost of Christmas Present warns Scrooge to beware both Ignorance and Want and explains that 'Ignorance' will bring doom to humankind through the wealthy people's indifference to the poor people's 'Want'. By presenting these creatures as children, Dickens suggests that these ills could be solved if society took responsibility; a modern reader understands that these problems still prevail today[11].

By the end of the novel, Scrooge has completed his journey towards redemption, guided by the supernatural. The spirits have instructed him, showing him the need for social responsibility, and have provided him with the chance to put right his past mistakes. This message resonates with both a contemporary and modern reader, perhaps showing us that if Scrooge can change, anyone can.

[9] **AO2**: clear understanding of how Dickens uses symbols to shape meaning and effect.

[10] **AO1**: further development of idea that supernatural forces are used to instruct Scrooge as he moves towards redemption.

[11] **AO3**: profound understanding of the impact of context on a modern reader's reactions.

Commentary

This is a critical, exploratory response that develops a relevant focus on the function of the ghosts and Scrooge's path to redemption. This is an answer based on profound insights, especially in relation to the concept of context. Insights into the relationship between language, form and meaning are clarified by a range of deftly chosen details.

DO IT!

Now use what you have learned to answer the following AQA exam-style question. Refer to the extract from Stave Two on page 14.

Starting with this extract, explore how Dickens presents ideas about guilt in *A Christmas Carol*.

Write about:

- how Dickens presents ideas about guilt in this extract
- how Dickens presents ideas about guilt in the novel as a whole.

[30 marks]

Read the following extract from Stave Four of *A Christmas Carol* and then answer the question that follows.

In this extract, Scrooge is taken to a graveyard by the Ghost of Christmas Yet to Come and makes a discovery.

> The Spirit was immovable as ever.
>
> Scrooge crept towards it, trembling as he went; and, following the finger, read upon the stone of the neglected grave his own name, EBENEZER SCROOGE.
>
> "Am *I* that man who lay upon the bed?" he cried upon his knees.
>
> The finger pointed from the grave to him, and back again.
>
> "No, Spirit! Oh no, no!"
>
> The finger still was there.
>
> "Spirit!" he cried, tight clutching at its robe, "Hear me! I am not the man I was. I will not be the man I must have been but for this intercourse. Why show me this, if I am past all hope?"
>
> For the first time the hand appeared to shake.
>
> "Good Spirit," he pursued, as down upon the ground he fell before it: "your nature intercedes for me, and pities me. Assure me that I yet may change these shadows you have shown me by an altered life?"
>
> The kind hand trembled.
>
> "I will honour Christmas in my heart, and try to keep it all the year. I will live in the Past, the Present, and the Future. The Spirits of all Three shall strive within me. I will not shut out the lessons that they teach. Oh, tell me I may sponge away the writing on this stone!"
>
> In his agony, he caught the spectral hand. It sought to free itself, but he was strong in his entreaty, and detained it. The Spirit, stronger yet, repulsed him.
>
> Holding up his hands in a last prayer to have his fate reversed, he saw an alteration in the Phantom's hood and dress. It shrunk, collapsed, and dwindled down into a bedpost.

Starting with this extract, explore how Dickens presents the idea of change in *A Christmas Carol*.

Write about:

* how Dickens presents the idea of change in this extract
* how Dickens presents the idea of change in the novel as a whole.

[30 marks]

Zoom in on the question

Starting with this extract, explore how Dickens presents the idea of change in *A Christmas Carol*.

Write about:

- how Dickens presents the idea of change in this extract
- how Dickens presents the idea of change in the novel as a whole.

First focus on the extract to 'anchor' the answer and to explore details about change. (AO1/AO2)

Concentrate on Dickens' ideas about how Scrooge changes and how he chooses language to present those ideas, for example, change inspired by self-interest. (AO1/AO2)

Stay relevant to the question focus: how and why Scrooge changes by the end of the novel. (AO2)

Start with the extract but clarify/ explain details here with references to other parts of the novel. (AO1/AO2)

Here are some ideas that could be included in an answer so as to cover the Assessment Objectives (AOs).

AO1 Consider how Scrooge is portrayed at the start of the novel as 'cold' and why he needs to change. Discuss how Scrooge transforms through the visions. Explore the idea of redemption and Scrooge's path to it: how is he different at the end of the novel? Examine lessons learned in Stave Four.

AO2 Explore **imagery** of the Ghost's transformation to the bedpost. Examine the turning points that lead to Scrooge's change/transformation, for example, regret towards the carol singer, regret for his loss of Belle and his sister, seeing the love within a family without wealth, fear of being forgotten.

AO3 Explore Dickens' message of social responsibility. How can the ghosts be viewed from a Christian viewpoint as saving us and ensuring we confess our sins?

A student has decided to focus on how far self-interest plays a part in Scrooge's redemption. This is the plan they have made to answer the question.

Paragraph	Content		Timing
I	Intro – use the question prep to establish focus of answer.		9.40
2	Extract shows a key moment when Scrooge's transformation can be seen: a turning point.		9.43
3	Do his actions come from self-interest? Marley finds the error of his ways in death and Scrooge finally commits to change due to facing his own death in the extract.	Refer back to extract and focus of the question throughout. Consider what Dickens might want the reader to think about change.	9.58
4	Extract as the end of this journey with the spirits. Redemption as a long and complex process.		10.06
5	Others showing Scrooge how he needs to change and why.		10.14
6	Conclusion – brief return to question. Are these lessons relevant today?		10.22

The essay plan above will meet these Assessment Objectives:

AO1 Read, understand and respond	Introduce the idea of redemption. Discuss how Scrooge transforms throughout the novel through the ghosts' teachings. Examine Scrooge's lessons learned in Stave Four. Does this transformation stem largely from self-interest? Link back to Marley, who only found remorse and change in death.
AO2 Language, form and structure	Explore imagery of the Ghost's transformation to the bedpost following Scrooge's assertion that he now has an 'altered life'. Consider how Scrooge is portrayed at the start of the novel as miserly. Explore Scrooge's path to redemption.
AO3 Contexts	Dickens' message to society: through support and goodwill from others, we can and should transform ourselves if it improves society.

In *A Christmas Carol*, Dickens presents the importance and possibility of change[1]. In this extract from the end of the novel, Dickens shows that character change is a largely internal process prompted and guided by external motivations.

This extract presents a key turning point in Scrooge's transformation. His shock at the image of his own 'neglected grave' is evident as he exclaims, 'No Spirit! Oh no, no!' The cry conveys Scrooge's rejection of this projected future, moving him towards redemption[2]. Despite the repeated denial, with the exclaimed repetition of 'no', Dickens presents him 'upon his knees', suggesting that he believes what the spirits show him; he is also penitent and reduced in status through his pose. Scrooge's transformation can also be seen through the presentation of the spirit itself. It appears 'immovable as ever' at the start of the extract, and yet after Scrooge's realisation, 'the kind hand trembled', presumably in approval or sympathy[3]. The reader could consider that this 'altered' Scrooge stems from his fear of being forgotten or 'neglected' after his death, like his grave. It is this motivation, rooted in self-interest, that moves him to change.

As this change stems from the threat of Scrooge's own death, it can be argued that Scrooge's promised goodwill and generosity is merely a consequence of his wish to avoid a tormented afterlife. This view of the afterlife mirrors Marley's own need to change, as in death he finds 'No rest, no peace. Incessant torture of remorse'[4]. Here, the increasingly complex language conveys Marley's turbulent thoughts and regrets only now acknowledged by Marley because of his own suffering. Similarly, Dickens presents Scrooge's final transformation coming after seeing the vision of his 'neglected grave'. The reader could therefore **infer** that selfish motivations drive his actions[5] rather than a wish to relieve the suffering of others.

Throughout the novel, change is revealed as a lengthy and complex process through Dickens' use of a **cyclical** narrative and dual timescale[6]. This structure is notable through Scrooge's interactions with the 'portly gentlemen'. Indeed, in Stave One, Scrooge is short-tempered with these charity collectors, replying to their search for donations for the poor with the statement that 'If they would rather die...they had better do it, and decrease the surplus population'. To complete the circle, when Scrooge sees one of these gentlemen again in Stave Five, he donates generously, 'Not a farthing less', suggesting that generosity is now ingrained in Scrooge[7]. Whilst this transformation appears to be sudden, Dickens conveys how internally the transformation has been a complex, challenging and lengthy process through the use of a dual timeline: whilst the physical

---

[1] **AO1:** clear opening, using words from the question to ensure relevance.

[2] **AO1:** precise choice of details to support points.

[3] **AO1/AO2:** precise language analysis highlighting significance of small details of language choice.

[4] **AO2 (structure):** clear understanding of how development of action through the novel help Dickens to shape meaning and effect.

[5] **AO2:** insight into how meaning is implied by language choices.

[6] **AO2:** insight into Dickens' craft as a writer.

[7] **AO1:** precise choice of details to support points.

journey is one night, the **metaphorical** journey covers the span of a lifetime. As this extract marks the end of Scrooge's journey with the spirits, the ghost's collapse to a menial 'bedpost' conveys that this challenging transformation for Scrooge is final and decisive[8].

AO1: quotation explained well.

Whilst this transformation seems to be a self-motivated process, Dickens presents change as reliant on the teaching and example of others. This reliance on others to show the way is largely evident through the role of the three spirits. In the extract, the image of the 'kind hand' of the third spirit represents the guiding nature of their role. This guidance allows these spirits to point towards the good-natured people in Scrooge's life, such as Fezziwig who is a key example for Scrooge to follow[9]. Fezziwig's exclamatory joviality towards his two apprentices; 'Yo ho my boys!...No more work, tonight' conveys his clear kindness and Christmas spirit, in stark contrast to Scrooge's lack thereof in Stave One. Fezziwig's example to Scrooge shows Scrooge how he must change and the joy it will bring to his life. Therefore, it is by these examples from others that Scrooge is encouraged and able to change[10].

AO3: presentation of social message that we can learn goodwill from others.

Overall, Dickens shows the complexity behind transformation, showing it as a vital process (leading to a better, fairer society) through which personal change and increased happiness can be achieved, but one which relies on time, self-motivation and external guidance.

AO1/AO3: 'conceptual' approach – question focus viewed from the importance of social message and Scrooge's development.

Commentary

This answer is thoughtful, exploratory and effectively structured to make the central argument convincing. The answer holds to a clear and specific concept – that self-interest and external influences motivate Scrooge's transformation, and this is well supported by a range of precise references to the text. The answer shows a sophisticated appreciation of how language and form contribute to Dickens' purposes, and overall the answer demonstrates insights into how Dickens deliberately makes choices of character, language and form to develop meaning and effect.

DO IT!

Now use what you have learned to answer the following AQA exam-style question. Refer to the extract from Stave Four on page 18.

Starting with this moment in the novel, explore how Dickens creates a sense of surprise in *A Christmas Carol*.

Write about:

- how Dickens creates a sense of surprise in this extract

- how Dickens creates a sense of surprise in the novel as a whole.

[30 marks]

Question 5

Read the following extract from Stave Three of *A Christmas Carol* and then answer the question that follows.

In this extract, Scrooge looks at the ghost's robe and sees two children within its folds.

From the foldings of its robe it brought two children; wretched, abject, frightful, hideous, miserable. They knelt down at its feet, and clung upon the outside of its garment.

"Oh, Man! Look here! Look, look, down here!" exclaimed the Ghost.

They were a boy and girl. Yellow, meagre, ragged, scowling, wolfish; but prostrate, too, in their humility. Where graceful youth should have filled their features out, and touched them with its freshest tints, a stale and shrivelled hand, like that of age, had pinched, and twisted them, and pulled them into shreds. Where angels might have sat enthroned, devils lurked, and glared out menacing. No change, no degradation, no perversion of humanity, in any grade, through all the mysteries of wonderful creation, has monsters half so horrible and dread.

Scrooge started back, appalled. Having them shown to him in this way, he tried to say they were fine children, but the words choked themselves, rather than be parties to a lie of such enormous magnitude.

"Spirit! Are they yours?" Scrooge could say no more.

"They are Man's," said the Spirit, looking down upon them. "And they cling to me, appealing from their fathers. This boy is Ignorance. This girl is Want. Beware them both, and all of their degree, but most of all beware this boy, for on his brow I see that written which is Doom, unless the writing be erased. Deny it!" cried the Spirit, stretching out its hand towards the city. "Slander those who tell it ye! Admit it for your factious purposes, and make it worse. And bide the end!"

"Have they no refuge or resource?" cried Scrooge.

"Are there no prisons?" said the Spirit, turning on him for the last time with his own words. "Are there no workhouses?"

Starting with this extract, explore how Dickens presents attitudes to poverty and the poor in *A Christmas Carol*.

Write about:

- how Dickens presents attitudes to poverty and the poor in this extract

- how Dickens presents attitudes to poverty and the poor in the novel as a whole.

[30 marks]

Zoom in on the question

Starting with this extract, explore how Dickens presents attitudes to poverty and the poor in *A Christmas Carol*.

Write about:

- how Dickens presents attitudes to poverty and the poor in this extract

- how Dickens presents attitudes to poverty and the poor in the novel as a whole.

First focus on the extract to 'anchor' the answer and to explore details from the extract about Dickens' presentation of attitudes towards poverty and the poor. (AO1/AO2)

Stay relevant to the question focus: how Dickens analyses different attitudes towards poverty and the poor in society. (AO1)

Concentrate on Dickens' ideas and his language choices to present those ideas, eg Dickens' use of contrasts. (AO2)

Start with the extract but clarify/explain details here with references to other parts of the novel. (AO1/AO2)

Here are some ideas that could be included in an answer in order to cover the Assessment Objectives (AOs).

AO1 Explore the differences between wealthy and poor. Refer to Scrooge's impoverished upbringing; link to Belle and the breakdown of their engagement. Discuss Dickens' presentation of the poor in Stave Four – the 'beetling shop'.

AO2 Consider the characterisation of Ignorance and Want and the realities of poverty shown through language choices, eg loss of childhood innocence as 'yellowed'. Compare this picture (including language) of poverty with that of the Cratchits.

AO3 Explore injustices and inequalities of Victorian England – 1834 Poor Law and Thomas Malthus. Consider contemporary ideas about the 'deserving poor' and wealthy people's fear of the unscrupulous poor.

A student has decided to focus on how the rich viewed the poor. This is the plan they have made to answer the question.

Paragraph	Content		Timing
1	Intro – use the question prep to establish focus of answer.		9.40
2	How Dickens presents the perceptions of the rich towards the poor – 1834 Poor Law and Thomas Malthus. Link to Belle: money is viewed as being more important than love and joy.		9.43
3	The extract: Ignorance and Want and language associated with these characters. The realities of poverty showing the lack of control over it. Childhood innocence stripped from them as a result of the actions of the rich.	Refer back to extract and focus of the question throughout. Consider what Dickens might want the reader to think about poverty and the poor.	9.58
4	Cratchit family as the 'deserving poor'. The Cratchits represent those who are poor because of circumstance, not because they are lazy.		10.06
5	Dickens shows that change is possible and needs to come from the rich. He shows the allegorical message and sets an example for the reader to follow.		10.13
6	Conclusion – brief return to question. Are these lessons relevant today?		10.22

The essay plan above will meet these Assessment Objectives:

AO1 Read, understand and respond	Explore perceptions of the rich towards the poor, and the Cratchit family as the 'deserving poor'.
AO2 Language, form and structure	Discuss Ignorance and Want: the realities of poverty shown through Dickens' language choices to signal the loss of childhood innocence through poverty.
AO3 Contexts	Consider Dickens' message to society: change is possible and needs to come from the rich. Refer to historical context: 1834 Poor Law and Thomas Malthus.

In *A Christmas Carol*, Dickens presents a number of inequalities suffered by the poor and the physical impact of poverty in order to convey his social message **❶** that generosity towards the poor is more valuable than punishment.

By portraying the ways in which the rich view the poor, Dickens highlights class injustices and inequalities in Victorian England. In Stave One, for example, Dickens presents the contrasting viewpoints of Scrooge and the charity collectors **❷**. The difference is evident as the gentlemen assume that 'You [Scrooge] wish to be left anonymous?' in donation, whereas, in reality, Scrooge takes a hostile view of the poor in his belief that 'If they would rather die...they had better do it, and decrease the surplus population'. This stark contrast between the two viewpoints emphasises Scrooge's uncharitable nature and greed. Indeed, it is Scrooge's Malthusian beliefs, supporting the expansions of workhouses through the 1834 Poor Law, which Dickens uses his novel to reject **❸**. In Stave Two, we learn that Scrooge himself was able to rise up from poverty, as Belle states, 'Our contract is an old one. It was made when we were both poor and content to be so' **❹**. Dickens presents Scrooge, now wealthy, as representing those who are unable to empathise with poverty and the poor.

In this extract, the result of this greed is shockingly presented through the characters Ignorance and Want. 'Where angels might have sat enthroned', these children are 'Yellow, meagre, ragged', the sickness imagery conveying that their childhood innocence has been stripped from them before they had any chance to remove themselves from poverty **❺**. Dickens' use of contrasts – their youth distorted by 'a stale and shrivelled hand'; 'angels' replaced by 'devils' that 'lurked and, glared' – reinforces how society's children are forgotten and neglected by the wealthy. These children will become the adults in Stave Four who rob a dead man without remorse; Dickens issues a warning to society that these symbols of the ills of the world will bring 'Doom', as written on the forehead of Ignorance. Dickens further removes the façade that this is the fault of the poor, and shifts the blame to the ignorant rich, as the Ghost of Christmas Present uses his final **dialogue** to quote Scrooge's own words from Stave One back to him; 'Are there no prisons?'...'Are there no workhouses?'. Here, Dickens reveals the absurdity of Scrooge's views in Stave One **❻**.

Scrooge's misconceptions about the poor are further shown through the presentation of the Cratchit family as the 'deserving poor'. Scrooge defends his refusal to donate to charity in Stave One with the argument that 'I can't afford to make idle people merry'. Dickens' use of the **adjective** 'idle' signals that Scrooge believes that poverty exists due to laziness **❼**. Through the Cratchits, however, Dickens shows that poverty is a result of

❶ **AO1**: clear opening, using words from the question to ensure relevance, and summing up the whole answer.

❷ **AO2**: perceptive links between language choices and historical context.

❸ **AO3**: helpful inclusion of historical context to develop idea.

❹ **AO1**: references well chosen and introduced to illustrate point.

❺ **AO2**: insight into how meaning is implied by language choices.

❻ **AO1/AO2**: Precise language analysis highlighting significance of small details of language choice.

❼ **AO1**: precise choice of details to support points.

the hierarchical structures of the Victorian era rather than of laziness. The exclamation that Martha 'had a deal of work to finish up last night...and had to clear away this morning', even on Christmas day, reveals how the entire Cratchit family works to generate their meagre income. Throughout the novel they are portrayed as the 'deserving poor': good-hearted and grateful but lacking in wealth[8]. Therefore, Dickens clearly dispels the misconception that poverty exists due to 'idle people'.

[8] **AO2:** insight into Dickens' craft as a writer.

Dickens does, however, show that not everyone shares these misconceptions about the poor. In Stave One, two 'gentlemen', a term revealing a level of status and wealth, are raising money for the poor. Dickens presents them conveying opposing attitudes to Scrooge. In Stave Five, through Dickens' use of a cyclical narrative, we see Scrooge donating to the same gentlemen, "'And will you have the goodness" – here Scrooge whispered in his ear... "Not a farthing less."'[9] The use of 'goodness', signalling Christian values combined with 'whisper', to show his discretion, reveals the extent of Scrooge's redemption born out of selflessness, understanding of the poor and attitudinal change. Dickens sets out his allegorical message of generosity and understanding here.

[9] **AO2 (structure):** clear understanding of how development of action through the novel help Dickens to shape meaning and effect.

Overall, Dickens presents the negative and unjust attitudes towards poverty and the poor which were prominent in the Victorian era. However, he also portrays the truth of Victorian poverty, showing the possibility of and need for wider attitudinal change mirroring that of Scrooge.

Commentary

This is a vigorous and well-argued analysis of Dickens' presentation of poverty and the poor. The student has used varied references to support their **interpretation** of Dickens' social message. There is a clear and perceptive understanding of how **allegory** and historical contexts interplay with Dickens' presentation of social injustice. The answer usefully draws on subject terminology (for example, 'symbol', 'imagery') to support an exploration of how Dickens influences the reader. The comments on structural development and characterisation are precise, relevant and thoughtful.

DO IT!

Now use what you have learned to answer the following AQA exam-style question. Refer to the extract from Stave Three on page 22.

Starting with this extract, explore how Dickens presents ideas about social responsibility in *A Christmas Carol*.

Write about:

• how Dickens presents ideas about social responsibility in this extract

• how Dickens presents ideas about social responsibility in the novel as a whole.

[30 marks]

Read the following extract from Stave Three of *A Christmas Carol* and then answer the question that follows.

The Ghost of Christmas Present and Scrooge visit a street where people are preparing for Christmas.

> Nor was it that the figs were moist and pulpy, or that the French plums blushed in modest tartness from their highly-decorated boxes, or that everything was good to eat and in its Christmas dress; but the customers were all so hurried and so eager in the hopeful promise of the day, that they tumbled up against each other at the door, crashing their wicker baskets wildly, and left their purchases upon the counter, and came running back to fetch them, and committed hundreds of the like mistakes, in the best humour possible; while the Grocer and his people were so frank and fresh, that the polished hearts with which they fastened their aprons behind might have been their own, worn outside for general inspection, and for Christmas daws to peck at if they chose.
>
> But soon the steeples called good people all to church and chapel, and away they came, flocking through the streets in their best clothes, and with their gayest faces. And at the same time there emerged, from scores of by-streets, lanes and nameless turnings, innumerable people, carrying their dinners to the bakers' shops. The sight of these poor revellers appeared to interest the Spirit very much, for he stood with Scrooge beside him in a baker's doorway, and, taking off the covers as their bearers passed, sprinkled incense on their dinners from his torch. And it was a very uncommon kind of torch, for once or twice, when there were angry words between some dinner-carriers who had jostled each other, he shed a few drops of water on them from it, and their good humour was restored directly. For they said, it was a shame to quarrel upon Christmas Day. And so it was! God love it, so it was!
>
> In time the bells ceased, and the bakers were shut up; and yet there was a genial shadowing forth of all these dinners and the progress of their cooking, in the thawed blotch of wet above each baker's oven; where the pavement smoked as if its stones were cooking too.
>
> "Is there a peculiar flavour in what you sprinkle from your torch?" asked Scrooge.
>
> "There is. My own."
>
> "Would it apply to any kind of dinner on this day?" asked Scrooge.
>
> "To any kindly given. To a poor one most."
>
> "Why to a poor one most?" asked Scrooge.
>
> "Because it needs it most."

Starting with this extract, explore how Dickens presents the spirit of Christmas in *A Christmas Carol*.

Write about:

*   how Dickens presents the spirit of Christmas in this extract

*   how Dickens presents the spirit of Christmas in the novel as a whole.

[30 marks]

Zoom in on the question

Starting with this extract, explore how Dickens presents the spirit of Christmas in *A Christmas Carol*.

Write about:

- how Dickens presents the spirit of Christmas in this extract
- how Dickens presents the spirit of Christmas in the novel as a whole.

First focus on the extract to 'anchor' the answer and to explore details about Dickens' presentation of the spirit of Christmas. (AO1/AO2)

Concentrate on Dickens' ideas and how he chooses his words to present those ideas, eg language of celebration. (AO2)

Stay relevant to the question focus: how Dickens shows that Christmas is an unusual time of the year. (AO1)

Start with the extract but clarify/explain details here with references to other parts of the novel. (AO1/AO2)

Here are some ideas that could be included in an answer in order to cover the Assessment Objectives (AOs).

AO1 Explore how Scrooge is shown as rejecting Christmas at the start of the novel and how Christmas 'saves' Scrooge and leads to his redemption. Consider how Scrooge's rejection of Christmas leads him to become 'cold' and miserly. This ultimately leads to his fate in Stave Four.

AO2 Discuss the role of Fred as the spirit of Christmas, and the role of family – explore the language of heat and cold. How does Dickens' use of language show the connection between joy and Christmas?

AO3 Comment on the role of Christmas in bringing people together in warmth and generosity: Christmas is celebrated by all people – wealthy and poor.

A student has decided to focus on how Christmas leads Scrooge towards redemption.

Paragraph	Content		Timing
1	Intro – use the question prep to establish focus of answer.		9.40
2	Christmas bringing people together in warmth and generosity. Simple acts seem more significant when infused with the spirit of Christmas. Changes of attitude and joy because of Christmas spirit.		9.43
3	Scrooge at start of novel – Malthus ideology, 'If they would rather die...they had better do it, and decrease the surplus population'. Contrast between this and the spirit's generosity in the extract. The social and moral message: importance of community.	Refer back to extract and focus of the question throughout. Consider what Dickens might want the reader to think about the spirit of Christmas.	9.58
4	The embodiment of Christmas through Fred and the Ghost of Christmas Present (see extract).		10.06
5	Christmas enabling Scrooge's redemption, role of Fred, generosity and selflessness within this; changing attitudes towards the Cratchits.		10.14
6	Conclusion – brief return to question. Are these lessons relevant today?		10.22

The essay plan above will meet these Assessment Objectives:

AO1 Read, understand and respond	Explore the idea that Christmas brings people together in warmth and generosity, and how simple acts seem even greater when infused with the spirit of Christmas. Refer to changes of attitude and joy because of Christmas spirit.
AO2 Language, form and structure	Discuss the embodiment of Christmas through Fred and the Ghost of Christmas Present. Refer to Fred's use of language of warmth and joy. Consider structure: Fred sets out the values of Christmas in Stave One and doesn't waver from them throughout the text.
AO3 Contexts	Discuss Scrooge at start of novel and his Malthusian view, 'If they would rather die...they had better do it, and decrease the surplus population'. Explore the social and moral message: the importance of community.

In this extract, Dickens presents the goodwill and values of Christmas; notably the generosity and communal spirit which is rooted in the celebration❶. Through the prominence of this **theme**, Dickens emphasises the importance of the values of Christmas and suggests that these values should extend beyond the occasion itself.

Dickens presents the importance of community in the spirit of Christmas, as it brings people together in warmth and generosity. As the extract opens with 'scores of by-streets, lanes, and nameless turnings, innumerable people', the vital importance of community is shown❷. The **rule of three** of the 'by-streets, lanes, and nameless turnings' makes the community seem bigger when infused with Christmas spirit. Dickens' cyclical structure furthers the presentation of the spirit of Christmas, its impacts being revealed as the story develops. Mirroring Scrooge's process of redemption as he gains deeper understanding of Christmas, the extravagance of the endless list of 'turkeys, geese, game, poultry...' at the start of Stave Three is revealed to have a spiritual meaning in this extract. Here, the ghost acts as the embodiment of Christmas, infusing the dinners of passers-by with his own 'flavour', which creates increased love and compassion❸. The monosyllabic 'My own', in the extract, suggests that this love and compassion is a simple attitudinal change brought by the Christmas spirit: Dickens suggests that this depends on the simple, but vital, values of community and generosity.

By contrasting the spirit of Christmas and Scrooge's initial beliefs, Dickens shows the social message behind these Christmas values. In Stave One, Scrooge abides by the views of Thomas Malthus, arguing that 'if they [the poor] would rather die...they had better do it, and decrease the surplus population'❹. In stark contrast, the spirit's generosity in this extract, giving incense 'To a poor one most', represents the social message of the importance of charity, understanding and generosity towards the people who need it most. The impact of these values is evident through the contrast between the 'good humour' of the community in the extract and the misery of Scrooge shown through the simile 'solitary as an oyster' in Stave One❺. Dickens shows how the spirit of Christmas can bring generosity to the community and joy to the individual.

Dickens further presents the spirit of Christmas through the characters which embody it – notably, Fred, who in his first line of dialogue, exclaims 'A merry Christmas, uncle!', thus setting out his view of Christmas from the start and from which he never wavers. His loyalty to these views is evident through his shock that his uncle refuses to 'Keep it!'. Fred's shock, shown by the **plosive** 'keep', conveys his strident determination and

① **AO1**: clear opening, using words from the question to ensure relevance.

② **AO1/AO2**: precise language analysis highlighting significance of small details of language choice.

③ **AO1**: precise choice of details to support points.

④ **AO1/**AO3: 'conceptual' approach – question focus viewed from perspective of Dickens' purpose.

⑤ **AO2** (structure): clear understanding of how development of action through the novel help Dickens to shape meaning and effect.

generosity in line with the spirit of Christmas[6]. This communal spirit is mirrored in the extract, as the 'genial shadowing' remains after 'the bakers were shut up'. This immortality of the spirit of Christmas is further shown by the Ghost of Christmas Present, who 'on its head [it] wore no other covering than a holly wreath'. Whilst this wreath could be a reference to the Biblical teachings of Christmas, it could also symbolise the cyclical spirit of Christmas – as eternal and vital[7].

The impact of the spirit of Christmas is evident through Scrooge's redemption. Mirroring the spirit in the extract, as he 'sprinkled incense on their dinners from his torch', Scrooge embraces the spirit of Christmas in Stave Five through his generous act of sending a turkey 'twice the size of Tiny Tim' to the Cratchit household[8]. The impact this increased generosity has on Scrooge himself is evident through the simile that he was 'as light as a feather' in Stave Five, in stark contrast to the image of his 'neglected grave' in Stave Four[9]. It is thus evident that Scrooge's happiness and redemption are due to him embracing the spirit of Christmas, clearly displaying Dickens' social message of the importance of these values in everyday life.

Overall, the spirit of Christmas is presented as being one of generosity, a sense of community and goodwill, in both this extract and throughout the text. Dickens shows the importance of the values of generosity and sharing, not just at Christmas but all year round, through Scrooge's redemption and the joy that Christmas brings in the extract[10].

[6] AO2: insight into how meaning is implied by language choices.

[7] AO2: insight into Dickens' craft as a writer.

[8] AO1: references well chosen and introduced to illustrate point.

[9] AO2 (structure): clear understanding of how development of action through the novel help Dickens to shape meaning and effect.

[10] AO3: perceptive reference to Dickens' key message.

Commentary

This is a perceptive, well-informed and carefully developed answer that successfully adopts an exploratory and critical approach to the novel and Dickens' intentions. The answer draws on wide-ranging references to support the interpretation of the ways Dickens presents his social message. Knowledge and understanding of the historical context of the novel enrich the analysis, giving rise to some sharp critical insights into the novel's likely effect on the reader. Subject terminology is used helpfully in support of these insights.

DO IT!

Now use what you have learned to answer the following AQA exam-style question. Refer to the extract from Stave Three on page 26.

Starting with this extract, explore how Dickens presents the ghosts as messengers of social change in *A Christmas Carol*.

Write about:

- how Dickens presents the ghosts as messengers of social change in this extract
- how Dickens presents the ghosts as messengers of change in the novel as a whole.

[30 marks]

Question 7

Read the following extract from Stave Three of *A Christmas Carol* and then answer the question that follows.

In this extract, the Ghost of Christmas Present leads Scrooge to the Cratchit's house, where they are sitting down to eat their Christmas meal.

Such a bustle ensued that you might have thought a goose the rarest of all birds; a feathered phenomenon, to which a black swan was a matter of course – and, in truth it was something very like it in that house. Mrs Cratchit made the gravy (ready beforehand in a little saucepan) hissing hot; Master Peter mashed the potatoes with incredible vigour; Miss Belinda sweetened up the apple-sauce; Martha dusted the hot plates; Bob took Tiny Tim beside him in a tiny corner at the table; the two young Cratchits set chairs for everybody, not forgetting themselves, and mounting guard upon their posts, crammed spoons into their mouths, lest they should shriek for goose before their turn came to be helped. At last the dishes were set on, and grace was said. It was succeeded by a breathless pause, as Mrs Cratchit, looking slowly all along the carving-knife, prepared to plunge it in the breast; but when she did, and when the long-expected gush of stuffing issued forth, one murmur of delight arose all round the board, and even Tiny Tim, excited by the two young Cratchits, beat on the table with the handle of his knife, and feebly cried "Hurrah!"

There never was such a goose. Bob said he didn't believe there ever was such a goose cooked. Its tenderness and flavour, size and cheapness, were the themes of universal admiration. Eked out by the apple-sauce and mashed potatoes, it was a sufficient dinner for the whole family; indeed, as Mrs Cratchit said with great delight (surveying one small atom of a bone upon the dish), they hadn't ate it all at last! Yet every one had had enough, and the youngest Cratchits, in particular, were steeped in sage and onion to the eyebrows! But now, the plates being changed by Miss Belinda, Mrs Cratchit left the room alone – too nervous to bear witnesses – to take the pudding up, and bring it in.

Starting with this extract, how far do you agree with the opinion that Dickens' presentation of the Cratchit family is unrealistic and sentimental in *A Christmas Carol*?

Write about:

- how Dickens presents the Cratchit family in this extract
- how Dickens presents the Cratchit family in the novel as a whole.

[30 marks]

Zoom in on the question

> Starting with this extract, how far do you agree with the opinion that Dickens' presentation of the Cratchit family is unrealistic and sentimental in *A Christmas Carol*?
>
> Write about:
>
> - how Dickens presents the Cratchit family in this extract
>
> - how Dickens presents the Cratchit family in the novel as a whole.

First focus on the extract to 'anchor' the answer and to explore details from the extract about Dickens' presentation of the Cratchit family. (AO1/AO2)

Concentrate on Dickens' ideas and his language choices to present those ideas. (AO1/AO2)

Stay relevant to the question focus: how far you agree with the opinion about Dickens' presentation of the Cratchit family. (AO1)

Start with the extract but clarify/explain details here with references to other parts of the novel. (AO1/AO2)

Here are some ideas that could be included in an answer in order to cover the Assessment Objectives (AOs).

AO1 Explore the family scenes with the Cratchit family at the start of the novel and Dickens' key social messages. Is the family presented as realistic or sentimental?

AO2 Consider key messages around the power of family love, eg the language used to describe the young Cratchits and the language used to describe the food. How are poverty and the poor described elsewhere in the novel, for example, with Ignorance and Want in Stave Three?

AO3 Explore how Dickens presents the Cratchit family as representing the 'deserving poor' – teaching the need for social responsibility by the wealthy. Consider how the Cratchit family are able to survive because of Scrooge at the end of the novel and Dickens' key messages to the wealthy.

This student has chosen to focus on the presentation of the Cratchits as unrealistic and sentimental. This is the plan they have made to answer the question.

Paragraph	Content		Timing
1	Intro – use the question prep to establish focus of answer.		9.40
2	Grateful nature of the family despite having little. Comparison to the wealthy reader. How the family's hardships are established.		9.43
3	Family values – love and goodwill. Glosses over potential family disputes to create a *sense* of idealism that the reader can admire and grieve for.	Refer back to extract and focus of the question throughout. Consider what Dickens might want the reader to think about the Cratchit family.	9.58
4	Purpose of this presentation – for wealthy reader, idealised version of reality. Comparison of Cratchits to the reality of Victorian poverty.		10.06
5	Unrealistic version of the poorer sector of Victorian society intended to evoke sympathy in the reader to aid Dickens' social message.		10.14
6	Conclusion – brief return to question. Are these lessons relevant today?		10.22

The essay plan above will meet these Assessment Objectives:

AO1 Read, understand and respond	Discuss how the family are grateful despite their hardships – comparison to the wealthy readership. Consider the scene as an idealised version of the reality of poverty and the poor.
AO2 Language, form and structure	Explore the language used to show family values, love and goodwill. Compare Martha and Bob Cratchit's love to the reality of poverty in Victorian England.
AO3 Contexts	Discuss how the idealised version of a poor family is intended to evoke sympathy in the reader to deliver Dickens' social message.

In *A Christmas Carol*, the Cratchits play a key role in the allegorical purpose of the novel, emphasising goodwill despite their poverty, and establishing a key example of the necessity of generosity[1]. However, in order to emphasise the hardships of the poor to the wealthy in society, Dickens' sentimental presentation of the family lacks the reality of family struggles and dynamics.

In this extract, Dickens presents the Cratchit family as kind and grateful, despite them having little. At the start of the extract, 'Such a bustle ensued that you might have thought a goose the rarest of all birds'. The use of the direct address, 'you', shows the largely wealthy readership that the Cratchits are grateful for what they have in spite of the simplicity of their 'goose' in comparison to the reader's own Christmas dinner[2].

Although their meal is seemingly meagre and simple, by the end of the extract 'every one had had enough': this simple statement is a further demonstration of the Cratchit's gratitude, through which Dickens perhaps distorts the realities of poverty in order to appeal to the reader's sympathy[3]. Indeed, by portraying a Christmas with traditional dinner and religious emphasis – as 'grace was said' – Dickens points to the similarities between the Cratchits' and the wealthy reader's celebrations. However, the differences – highlighted by the 'cheapness' of the goose and the small amount of meat suggested by 'eked out by apple sauce' – show that, although the celebrations may be the same in essence, they are different in quantity and quality. These details ensure that the reader remains sympathetic towards the Cratchits: we are moved by their insistence that their obviously sparse meal is a feast. The purpose of this depiction of family celebration is therefore to show the spirit of Christmas and the importance of generosity to contemporary readers, but it does not portray the reality of Victorian poverty[4].

The Cratchits also display the family values of love and generosity towards each other. Prior to this extract we see the large family coming together, as Martha hides on Bob Cratchit's return, but 'Martha didn't like to see him disappointed, if it were only in joke; so she came out prematurely from behind the closet door, and ran into his arms'. Their deep-rooted love is revealed in each added detail within the complex sentence structure[5]. In the extract, everyone good-naturedly waits their turn – the two young Cratchits even 'crammed spoons into their mouths, lest they should shriek for goose before their turn came to be helped'. The joyful language here creates for the reader a sense of the love, generosity and understanding amongst the family, which has even been instilled in its youngest members. However, this idealised version of family life glosses over potential family

1 AO1: clear opening, using words from the question to ensure relevance.

2 AO1/AO2: precise language analysis highlighting significance of small details of language choice.

3 AO1: precise choice of details to support points.

4 AO1/AO3: 'conceptual' approach – question focus viewed from perspective of Dickens' purpose and key message.

5 AO1/AO2: precise language analysis highlighting significance of small details of language choice.

disputes in order to create a sense of idealism and challenge the Victorian stereotype that the poor are lazy and undeserving[6].

The purpose of this idealised presentation of the Cratchit family is to evoke sympathy amongst his readers, who would largely be wealthy[7]. In vast contrast to the love and support within the family, is the image of Ignorance and Want at the end of Stave Three. At a time when children were seen as being the embodiment of purity, Ignorance and Want are 'Yellow, meagre, ragged'[8]. This **metaphor** and striking list of disturbing adjectives conveys the harsh reality of child poverty in Victorian England in stark contrast to the love and support within the Cratchit household[9].

The Cratchits are presented as a sentimental example of the poor in Victorian society. They are a tool for Dickens to convey his social message that the wealthy within society should be responsible for those in poverty. Through this sentimental portrayal of the 'deserving poor', Dickens' purpose was to evoke sympathy in the reader to aid his social message[10]. Hence, at the end of the novel, Tiny Tim is saved by Scrooge's generosity. With the last words of the novel, 'God bless us everyone', Tiny Tim and his reversed fate enable Dickens to link a Christian message with what he hopes for society[11].

Overall, the unyielding family values and gratitude within the Cratchit family are unrealistic and sentimental. This presentation does, however, reinforce the social message of the novel, creating sympathy amongst the wealthy contemporary reader, which may not have materialised had the family been portrayed in a more realistic light.

[6] AO2: insight into how meaning is implied by language choices.

[7] AO2: insight into Dickens' craft as a writer.

[8] AO1: references well chosen and introduced to illustrate point.

[9] AO2/AO3: perceptive links between language choices and historical context.

[10] AO3: helpful inclusion of historical context to develop idea.

[11] AO2/AO3: insight into how meaning and links to key messages are implied by language choices.

Commentary

This is a critical and perceptive response that develops a relevant and thorough answer to the question. This is a conceptualised answer based on sensitive insights into Dickens' presentation of the Cratchit family and how this presentation allows him to deliver his key social message. Some profound insights are based on a fine appreciation of language details and how Dickens guides our responses to the Cratchit family through the novel.

DO IT!

Now use what you have learned to answer the following AQA exam-style question. Refer to the extract from Stave Three on page 30.

Starting with this extract, explore how Dickens presents Christmas celebrations in *A Christmas Carol*.

Write about:

• how Dickens presents Christmas celebrations in this extract

• how Dickens presents Christmas celebrations in the novel as a whole.

[30 marks]

Question 8

Read the following extract from Stave Two of *A Christmas Carol* and then answer the question that follows.

In this extract, the Ghost of Christmas Past shows Scrooge a scene from his past.

> It opened; and a little girl, much younger than the boy, came darting in, and, putting her arms about his neck, and often kissing him, addressed him as her "dear, dear brother."
>
> "I have come to bring you home, dear brother!" said the child, clapping her tiny hands, and bending down to laugh. "To bring you home, home, home!"
>
> "Home, little Fan?" returned the boy.
>
> "Yes!" said the child, brimful of glee. "Home for good and all. Home for ever and ever. Father is so much kinder than he used to be, that home's like Heaven! He spoke so gently to me one dear night when I was going to bed, that I was not afraid to ask him once more if you might come home; and he said Yes, you should; and sent me in a coach to bring you. And you're to be a man!" said the child, opening her eyes, "and are never to come back here; but first we're to be together all the Christmas long, and have the merriest time in all the world."
>
> "You are quite a woman, little Fan!" exclaimed the boy.
>
> She clapped her hands and laughed, and tried to touch his head; but being too little, laughed again, and stood on tiptoe to embrace him. Then she began to drag him, in her childish eagerness, towards the door; and he, nothing loth to go, accompanied her.

Starting with this extract, explore how Dickens presents female characters in *A Christmas Carol*.

Write about:

- how Dickens presents Fan in this extract
- how Dickens presents female characters in the novel as a whole.

[30 marks]

Zoom in on the question

Starting with this extract, explore how Dickens presents female characters in *A Christmas Carol*.

Write about:

- how Dickens presents Fan in this extract
- how Dickens presents female characters in the novel as a whole.

First focus on the extract to 'anchor' the answer and to explore details from the extract about Dickens' presentation of Fan. (AO1/AO2)

Concentrate on Dickens' ideas and how he chooses his words to present those ideas, for example, women as home-makers. (AO1/AO2)

Stay relevant to the question focus: how Dickens presents female characters in the novel. (AO1)

Start with the extract but clarify/explain details here with references to other parts of the novel. (AO1/AO2)

Here are some ideas that could be included in an answer in order to cover the Assessment Objectives (AOs).

AO1 Explore the scenes with the Cratchit family women as home-makers. Explore the presentation of Fan and Belle; contrast with working-class women, eg, the laundress in Stave Four.

AO2 Consider women as support to men, eg, language used to describe Fan, language used to describe Scrooge's niece. How are women described elsewhere in the novel, for example, Belle in Stave Two?

AO3 Explore how Dickens presents Mrs Cratchit as home-maker and the expectations of women in Victorian society.

This student has chosen to focus on the presentation of women's role as a support to men. This is the plan they have made to answer the question.

Paragraph	Content		Timing
1	Intro – use the question prep to establish focus of answer.		9.40
2	Women's role as home-maker, for example, Mrs Cratchit. Women are not expected to mature or learn, for example, Fan – contrast with Scrooge's opportunities.		9.43
3	Household roles: women as wives and mothers who support the men around them. Men as head of the household.	Refer back to extract and focus of the question throughout. Consider what Dickens might want the reader to think about roles of the women in the novel.	9.58
4	Women and their role in Scrooge's redemption: Belle and Fan.		10.06
5	Women's role in the novel to bring joy to men.		10.14
6	Conclusion – brief return to question. Are these lessons relevant today?		10.22

The essay plan above will meet these Assessment Objectives:

AO1 Read, understand and respond	Discuss women's role as home-maker and support to men around them – to bring joy and to save men from their own weaknesses.
AO2 Language, form and structure	Consider the function of women in the novel: Belle and Fan and links to Scrooge's redemption. Explain how Belle, seen through older Scrooge's eyes, becomes part of his redemption process.
AO3 Contexts	Explore household roles and the role of women presented throughout the novel.

In *A Christmas Carol*, women are presented as a source of joy associated with the home. Whilst female characters play a role in Scrooge's redemption, they are shown as supporting characters without their own significance, thus mirroring the role of women in Victorian society❶.

The extract presents young women as of little significance, and as being primarily associated with the home rather than educational **settings**. This is shown by Fan, who is described not by her name but as a 'little girl', thereby diminishing her status and establishing her as a side character with 'little' significance. Whilst this could describe her youth rather than her gender, Scrooge states she is 'quite a woman' in spite of her 'childish eagerness', suggesting that women are not expected to mature or learn beyond this stage❷. Fan's home-making role in the novel is evident when she states that she has come 'To bring you home, home, home!' This quick repetition emphasises that 'home' is where Fan is from and where she will remain❸, contrasting with Scrooge's ability to leave to attend school – albeit unhappily. Here, Fan's situation mirrors women's limited opportunities to move beyond the home and access education in Victorian England.

Whilst some male characters in the novel, notably Scrooge, enjoy lives of power and enterprise, the role of the women is as wives and mothers, confined to the home. Even when Belle leaves Scrooge in Stave Two, she does this reasoning that 'I release you. With a full heart, for the love of him you once were'; the decisive monosyllables and a focus on 'love' showing that this decision is to benefit Scrooge❹. Further mirroring the 'little girl' in this extract, Mrs Cratchit is not introduced by her own name but rather as 'Cratchit's wife', creating a sense of male ownership through marriage, without autonomy of her own. Her role inside the home is evident, as Bob Cratchit regards the Christmas pudding as 'the greatest success achieved by Mrs Cratchit since their marriage'❺. She is the home-maker, whereas Bob Cratchit's role is leader and provider for the family, both usual roles in Victorian society. This contrast between men and women is depicted in the unseen but powerful 'Father' in the extract. When Fan says, 'he said Yes, you should', it is evident that Scrooge's father, as the man of the household, makes the key decisions❻.

The female characters in *A Christmas Carol* do, however, aid Scrooge's redemption (when the spirits play the scenes back to him) and retain opinions of their own. In the extract, this is shown through Fan's joyous spirit as she 'stood on tiptoe to embrace him', physically representing familial love and teaching Scrooge the value of this. Similarly, Belle plays a part in Scrooge's redemption, when the scene from his youth

❶ AO1/AO3: clear opening, using words from the question to ensure relevance and linking to historical context.

❷ AO1/AO2: precise language analysis highlighting significance of small details of language choice.

❸ AO1/AO2: precise choice of details to support points.

❹ AO1/AO2: 'conceptual' approach – question focus viewed from POV of women as a support to men.

❺ AO1/AO2: precise language analysis highlighting significance of small details of language choice.

❻ AO2: insight into how meaning is implied by language choices.

is presented to him: her decision to leave him shows what can be lost through greed when she argues that 'another idol has displaced me...a golden one'. The appeal of both Belle and Fan is clearly focused around pathos: they show the importance of emotion and love, thus reinforcing gender stereotypes[7].

Throughout the novel, the key role of women is to bring joy to the male characters. In the extract, this is shown through the happiness brought by Fan, who 'came darting in, and putting her arms about his neck, and often kissing him', this accumulating list emphasising the joy she brings to Scrooge, an otherwise 'solitary child, neglected by his friends'[7]. Similarly, 'Scrooge's niece', again notably introduced through her relation to the male characters, is seen as 'satisfactory' as she is 'exceedingly pretty with a 'ripe little mouth'. This description shows how 'Scrooge's niece' is viewed primarily as an object of male desire[8].

Overall, it is evident that women in the text, whist aiding Scrooge's transformation, are held back by both Victorian societal norms and the male characters in the novel. The assumption that female characters will have supporting roles as wives and mothers is never challenged by Dickens and their servitude is never included in the list of injustices portrayed in the novel[9].

[7] **AO1/AO3:** 'conceptual' approach – question focus viewed from POV of function of women as a support to men.

[7] **AO2:** insight into Dickens' craft as a writer.

[8] **AO1:** references are well chosen and introduced to illustrate point.

[9] **AO3:** helpful inclusion of historical context to develop idea.

Commentary

This is a passionate and well-argued analysis of Dickens' presentation of women in the novel. The student has used varied references to support their interpretation of the function of selected women in the novel. There is a clear and perceptive understanding of the historical context's interplay with Dickens' presentation of the role of women both in society and in the novel. The answer usefully draws on language analysis to support an exploration of how Dickens influences the reader. The comments on characterisation are original and thoughtful.

DO IT!

Now use what you have learned to answer the following AQA exam-style question.

Starting with this moment in the novel, explore how Dickens presents ideas about family and home life in *A Christmas Carol*.

Write about:

- how Dickens presents ideas about family and home life in this extract
- how Dickens presents ideas about family and home life in the novel as a whole.

[30 marks]

Read the following extract from Stave Five of *A Christmas Carol* and then answer the question that follows.

In this extract, Scrooge is waiting for Bob Cratchit to arrive at work after the Christmas celebrations.

"Hallo!" growled Scrooge in his accustomed voice as near as he could feign it. "What do you mean by coming here at this time of day?"

"I am very sorry, sir," said Bob. "I *am* behind my time."

"You are!" repeated Scrooge. "Yes. I think you are. Step this way, if you please."

"It's only once a year, sir," pleaded Bob, appearing from the Tank. "It shall not be repeated. I was making rather merry yesterday, sir."

"Now, I'll tell you what, my friend," said Scrooge. "I am not going to stand this sort of thing any longer. And therefore," he continued, leaping from his stool, and giving Bob such a dig in the waistcoat that he staggered back into the Tank again: "and therefore I am about to raise your salary!"

Bob trembled, and got a little nearer to the ruler. He had a momentary idea of knocking Scrooge down with it, holding him, and calling to the people in the court for help and a strait-waistcoat.

"A Merry Christmas, Bob!" said Scrooge, with an earnestness that could not be mistaken as he clapped him on the back. "A merrier Christmas, Bob, my good fellow, than I have given you for many a year! I'll raise your salary, and endeavour to assist your struggling family, and we will discuss your affairs this very afternoon, over a Christmas bowl of smoking bishop, Bob! Make up the fires and buy another coal-scuttle before you dot another 'i' Bob Cratchit!"

Scrooge was better than his word. He did it all, and infinitely more; and to Tiny Tim, who did *not* die, he was a second father. He became as good a friend, as good a master, and as good a man as the good old city knew, or any other good old city, town or borough in the good old world.

Starting with this moment in the novel, explore how Dickens presents Scrooge's journey towards redemption in *A Christmas Carol*.

Write about:

- Scrooge's journey towards redemption in this extract
- Scrooge's journey towards redemption in the novel as a whole.

[30 marks]

Exam-style question 2

Read the following extract from Stave Two of *A Christmas Carol* and then answer the question that follows.

In this extract, the Ghost of Christmas Present takes Scrooge to a place where he grew up.

The jocund travellers came on; and as they came, Scrooge knew and named them every one. Why was he rejoiced beyond all bounds to see them? Why did his cold eye glisten, and his heart leap up as they went past? Why was he filled with gladness when he heard them give each other Merry Christmas, as they parted at cross-roads and by-ways for their several homes? What was merry Christmas to Scrooge? Out upon merry Christmas! What good had it ever done to him?

"The school is not quite deserted," said the Ghost. "A solitary child, neglected by his friends, is left there still."

Scrooge said he knew it. And he sobbed.

They left the high road by a well-remembered lane, and soon approached a mansion of dull red brick, with a little weathercock-surmounted cupola on the roof and a bell hanging in it. It was a large house, but one of broken fortunes: for the spacious offices were little used, their walls were damp and mossy, their windows broken, and their gates decayed. Fowls clucked and strutted in the stables; and the coach-houses and sheds were overrun with grass. Nor was it more retentive of its ancient state within; for entering the dreary hall, and glancing through the open doors of many rooms, they found them poorly furnished, cold and vast. There was an earthy savour in the air, a chilly bareness in the place, which associated itself somehow with too much getting up by candle-light, and not too much to eat.

They went, the Ghost and Scrooge, across the hall, to a door at the back of the house. It opened before them, and disclosed a long, bare, melancholy room, made barer still by lines of plain deal forms and desks. At one of these a lonely boy was reading near a feeble fire; and Scrooge sat down upon a form, and wept to see his poor forgotten self as he used to be.

Starting with this moment in the novel, explore how Dickens presents ideas about childhood in *A Christmas Carol*.

Write about:

*   Dickens' ideas about childhood in this extract
*   Dickens' ideas about childhood in the novel as a whole.

[30 marks]

Exam-style question 3

Read the following extract from Stave Two of *A Christmas Carol* and then answer the question that follows.

In this extract, the Ghost of Christmas Present shows Scrooge a scene from his past.

He was not alone, but sat by the side of a fair young girl in a mourning dress: in whose eyes there were tears, which sparkled in the light that shone out of the Ghost of Christmas Past.

"It matters little," she said, softly. "To you, very little. Another idol has displaced me; and, if it can cheer and comfort you in time to come as I would have tried to do, I have no just cause to grieve."

"What Idol has displaced you?" he rejoined.

"A golden one."

"This is the even-handed dealing of the world!" he said. "There is nothing on which it is so hard as poverty; and there is nothing it professes to condemn with such severity as the pursuit of wealth!"

"You fear the world too much," she answered, gently. "All your other hopes have merged into the hope of being beyond the chance of its sordid reproach. I have seen your nobler aspirations fall off one by one, until the master passion, Gain, engrosses you. Have I not?"

"What then?" he retorted. "Even if I have grown so much wiser, what then? I am not changed towards you."

She shook her head.

"Am I?"

"Our contract is an old one. It was made when we were both poor, and content to be so, until, in good season, we could improve our worldly fortune by our patient industry. You *are* changed. When it was made, you were another man."

"I was a boy," he said impatiently.

"Your own feeling tells you that you were not what you are," she returned. "I am. That which promised happiness when we were one in heart is fraught with misery now that we are two. How often and how keenly I have thought of this I will not say. It is enough that I *have* thought of it, and can release you."

"Have I ever sought release?"

"In words. No. Never."

Starting with this moment in the novel, explore how Dickens presents ideas about the link between wealth and happiness in *A Christmas Carol*.

Write about:

- Dickens' ideas about wealth and happiness in this extract
- Dickens' ideas about wealth and happiness in the novel as a whole.

[30 marks]

Exam-style question 4

Read the following extract from Stave One of *A Christmas Carol* and then answer the question that follows.

In this extract, the ghost of Jacob Marley visits Scrooge.

Though he looked the phantom through and through, and saw it standing before him; though he felt the chilling influence of its death-cold eyes; and marked the very texture of the folded kerchief bound about its head and chin, which wrapper he had not observed before; he was still incredulous, and fought against his senses.

"How now!" said Scrooge, caustic and cold as ever. "What do you want with me?"

"Much!" – Marley's voice, no doubt about it.

"Who are you?"

"Ask me who I *was*."

"Who *were* you then?" said Scrooge, raising his voice. "You're particular – for a shade." He was going to say "*to* a shade," but substituted this, as more appropriate.

"In life I was your partner, Jacob Marley."

"Can you – can you sit down?" asked Scrooge, looking doubtfully at him.

"I can."

"Do it then."

Scrooge asked the question, because he didn't know whether a ghost so transparent might find himself in a condition to take a chair; and felt that, in the event of its being impossible, it might involve the necessity of an embarrassing explanation. But the Ghost sat down on the opposite side of the fireplace, as if he were quite used to it.

"You don't believe in me," observed the Ghost.

"I don't," said Scrooge.

"What evidence would you have of my reality beyond that of your own senses?"

"I don't know," said Scrooge.

"Why do you doubt your senses?"

"Because," said Scrooge, "a little thing affects them. A slight disorder of the stomach makes them cheats. You may be an undigested bit of beef, a blot of mustard, a crumb of cheese, a fragment of an underdone potato. There's more of gravy than of grave about you, whatever you are!"

Scrooge was not much in the habit of cracking jokes, nor did he feel in his heart by any means waggish then. The truth is, that he tried to be smart, as a means of distracting his own attention, and keeping down his terror; for the spectre's voice disturbed the very marrow in his bones.

Starting with this moment in the novel, explore how Scrooge uses humour and scorn to distract himself from the truth in *A Christmas Carol*.

Write about:

* how Scrooge uses humour and scorn in this extract
* how Scrooge uses humour and scorn in the novel as a whole.

[30 marks]

Read the following extract from Stave Three of *A Christmas Carol* and then answer the question that follows.

In this extract, the Ghost of Christmas Present takes Scrooge to see a family celebration at Christmas.

> "Indeed, I think he loses a very good dinner," interrupted Scrooge's niece. Everybody else said the same, and they must be allowed to have been competent judges, because they had just had dinner; and, with the dessert upon the table, were clustered round the fire, by lamplight.
>
> "Well! I'm very glad to hear it," said Scrooge's nephew, "because I haven't great faith in these young housekeepers. What do *you* say, Topper?"
>
> Topper had clearly got his eye upon one of Scrooge's niece's sisters, for he answered that a bachelor was a wretched outcast, who had no right to express an opinion on the subject. Whereat Scrooge's niece's sister – the plump one with the lace tucker, not the one with the roses – blushed.
>
> "Do go on, Fred," said Scrooge's niece, clapping her hands. "He never finishes what he begins to say! He is such a ridiculous fellow!"
>
> Scrooge's nephew revelled in another laugh, and, as it was impossible to keep the infection off, though the plump sister tried hard to do it with aromatic vinegar, his example was unanimously followed.
>
> "I was only going to say," said Scrooge's nephew, "that the consequence of his taking a dislike to us, and not making merry with us, is, as I think, that he loses some pleasant moments, which could do him no harm. I am sure he loses pleasanter companions than he can find in his own thoughts, either in his mouldy old office, or his dusty chambers. I mean to give him the same chance every year, whether he likes it or not, for I pity him. He may rail at Christmas till he dies, but he can't help thinking better of it – I defy him – if he finds me going there in good temper, year after year, and saying, 'Uncle Scrooge, how are you?' If it only puts him in the vein to leave his poor clerk fifty pounds, *that's* something; and I think I shook him yesterday."
>
> It was their turn to laugh, now, at the notion of his shaking Scrooge. But, being thoroughly good-natured, and not much caring what they laughed at, so that they laughed at any rate, he encouraged them in their merriment, and passed the bottle joyously.

Starting with this moment in the novel, explore how Dickens presents family relationships in *A Christmas Carol*.

Write about:

- how Dickens presents family relationships in this extract

- how Dickens presents family relationships in the novel as a whole.

[30 marks]

Read the following extract from Stave Four of *A Christmas Carol* and then answer the question that follows.

In this extract, the Ghost of Christmas Yet to Come takes Scrooge to come to listen to a conversation between a group of businessmen.

> "No," said a great fat man with a monstrous chin, "I don't know much about it, either way. I only know he's dead."
>
> "When did he die?" enquired another.
>
> "Last night, I believe."
>
> "Why, what was the matter with him?" asked a third, taking a vast quantity of snuff out of a very large snuff-box. "I thought he'd never die."
>
> "God knows," said the first with a yawn.
>
> "What has he done with his money?" asked a red-faced gentleman with a pendulous excrescence on the end of his nose, that shook like the gills of a turkey-cock.
>
> "I haven't heard," said the man with the large chin, yawning again. "Left it to his company, perhaps. He hasn't left it to *me*. That's all I know."
>
> This pleasantry was received with a general laugh.
>
> "It's likely to be a very cheap funeral," said the same speaker; "for upon my life, I don't know of anybody to go to it. Suppose we make up a party and volunteer?"
>
> "I don't mind going if a lunch is provided," observed the gentleman with the excrescence on his nose. "But I must be fed if I make one."
>
> Another laugh.
>
> "Well, I am the most disinterested among you, after all," said the first speaker, "for I never wear black gloves, and I never eat lunch. But I'll offer to go if anybody else will. When I come to think of it, I'm not at all sure that I wasn't his most particular friend; for we used to stop and speak whenever we met. Bye, bye!"
>
> Speakers and listeners strolled away, and mixed with other groups. Scrooge knew the men, and looked towards the Spirit for an explanation.

Starting with this moment in the novel, explore how Dickens presents the world of business in *A Christmas Carol*.

Write about:

- how Dickens presents the world of business in this extract

- how Dickens presents the world of business in the novel as a whole.

[30 marks]

Read the following extract from Stave Four of *A Christmas Carol* and then answer the question that follows.

The Ghost of Christmas Yet to Come has taken Scrooge to a shop where a woman is selling a dead man's blankets and shirt.

"His blankets?" asked Joe.

"Whose else's do you think?" replied the woman. "He isn't likely to take cold without 'em, I dare say."

"I hope he didn't die of anything catching? Eh?" said old Joe, stopping in his work, and looking up.

"Don't you be afraid of that," returned the woman. "I an't so fond of his company that I'd loiter about him for such things, if he did. Ah! You may look through that shirt till your eyes ache; but you won't find a hole in it, nor a threadbare place. It's the best he had, and a fine one too. They'd have wasted it, if it hadn't been for me."

"What do you call wasting of it?" asked old Joe.

"Putting it on him to be buried in, to be sure," replied the woman with a laugh. "Somebody was fool enough to do it, but I took it off again. If calico an't good enough for such a purpose, it isn't good enough for anything. It's quite as becoming to the body. He can't look uglier than he did in that one."

Scrooge listened to this dialogue in horror. As they sat grouped about their spoil, in the scanty light afforded by the old man's lamp, he viewed them with a detestation and disgust which could hardly have been greater, though they had been obscene demons, marketing the corpse itself.

"Ha, ha!" laughed the same woman when old Joe, producing a flannel bag with money in it, told out their several gains upon the ground. "This is the end of it, you see! He frightened every one away from him when he was alive, to profit us when he was dead! Ha, ha, ha!"

"Spirit!" said Scrooge, shuddering from head to foot. "I see, I see. The case of this unhappy man might be my own. My life tends that way now. Merciful Heaven, what is this?"

Starting with this moment in the novel, explore how Dickens presents greed in *A Christmas Carol*.

Write about:

- how Dickens presents greed in this extract
- how Dickens presents greed in the novel as a whole.

[30 marks]

Read the following extract from Stave Three of *A Christmas Carol* and then answer the question that follows.

In this extract, the Ghost of Christmas Present shows Scrooge a scene from the Cratchit household. Bob Cratchit returns home and his daughter, Martha, plays a joke on him.

> So Martha hid herself, and in came little Bob, the father, with at least three feet of comforter, exclusive of the fringe, hanging down before him; and his threadbare clothes darned up and brushed to look seasonable; and Tiny Tim upon his shoulder. Alas for Tiny Tim, he bore a little crutch, and had his limbs supported by an iron frame!
>
> "Why, where's our Martha?" cried Bob Cratchit, looking round.
>
> "Not coming," said Mrs Cratchit.
>
> "Not coming!" said Bob, with a sudden declension in his high spirits; for he had been Tim's blood horse all the way from church, and had come home rampant. "Not coming upon Christmas Day!"
>
> Martha didn't like to see him disappointed, if it were only in joke; so she came out prematurely from behind the closet door, and ran into his arms, while the two young Cratchits hustled Tiny Tim, and bore him off into the wash-house, that he might hear the pudding singing in the copper.
>
> "And how did little Tim behave?" asked Mrs Cratchit when she had rallied Bob on his credulity and Bob had hugged his daughter to his heart's content.
>
> "As good as gold," said Bob, "and better. Somehow he gets thoughtful sitting by himself so much, and thinks the strangest things you ever heard. He told me, coming home, that he hoped the people saw him in the church, because he was a cripple, and it might be pleasant to them to remember upon Christmas Day who made lame beggars walk and blind men see."
>
> Bob's voice was tremulous when he told them this, and trembled more when he said that Tiny Tim was growing strong and hearty.
>
> His active little crutch was heard upon the floor, and back came Tiny Tim before another word was spoken, escorted by his brother and sister to his stool beside the fire; and while Bob, turning up his cuffs – as if, poor fellow, they were capable of being made more shabby – compounded some hot mixture in a jug with gin and lemons, and stirred it round and round, and put it on the hob to simmer, Master Peter and the two ubiquitous young Cratchits went to fetch the goose, with which they soon returned in high procession.

Starting with this moment in the novel, explore how Dickens presents Bob Cratchit in *A Christmas Carol*.

Write about:

• how Dickens presents Bob Cratchit in this extract

• how Dickens presents Bob Cratchit in the novel as a whole.

[30 marks]

Glossary

adjective A word that provides information about a noun.

allegory (allegorical) A narrative (or image) that can be interpreted to reveal a hidden meaning. This meaning is usually a moral or political lesson.

context The context of a poem, play, novel or story is the set of conditions in which it was written. These might include: the writer's life; society, habits and beliefs at the time they wrote; an event that influenced the writing; and the genre of the writing. The context is also seen in terms of influences on the reader, so, for example, a modern audience would see a Dickens novel differently from audiences in his own time, as their life experiences would be different.

cyclical (structure) The structure is described as cyclical when it ends at a similar point to the beginning.

dialogue The words that characters say in plays or in **fiction**. In fiction, these words are usually shown within inverted commas ('…').

effect The impact of a writer's words on a reader: how the words create a mood, feeling or reaction.

evidence Details or clues that support a point of view. A quotation can be a form of evidence in which a few words are copied from a text to support a point of view.

foil A character that provides a contrast with another character, often to show their good qualities.

imagery The 'pictures' a writer puts into the reader's mind. **Similes** and **metaphors** are particular forms of imagery. We also talk about violent, graphic or religious imagery, and so on.

infer (inference) To 'read between the lines'; to work out meaning from clues in the text. When we infer, we are making an inference.

language (choices) The words and the **style** that a writer chooses in order to have an **effect** on a reader.

metaphor (metaphorical) Comparing two things by referring to them as though they are the same thing (for example: His face *was a thunder cloud*. The boy *was an angry bear*).

monosyllable/monosyllabic Consisting of one syllable/speaking in words of one syllable.

narrator The person who tells the story. A *first person narrator* tells the story as though it is happening to them personally (for example: *I* walked slowly down the street). A *third person narrator* tells the story from someone else's point of view (for example: *He* walked slowly down the street).

plot The plot of a literary text is the *story* – the narrative – or an interrelated series of events as described by the author.

plosive A speech sound: t, k, and p (voiceless) and d, g, and b (voiced).

point of view (POV) See **viewpoint**.

quotation A word, phrase, sentence or passage copied from a text, usually used to support an argument or point of view. A quotation should be surrounded by inverted commas ('…'). It is usually wise to make quotations as short as possible, sometimes just one well-chosen word is enough.

rule of three A pattern of three characters, events or descriptions to create a literary effect.

setting The setting is the *time and place* in which a play or story takes place. The setting could also include the social and political circumstances (or **context**) of the action.

simile Comparing two things using either the word *like* or *as* (for example: The boy was *like an angry bear*. His running was *as loud as thunder*. Her face was *as yellow as custard*).

stave A verse of a song.

structure How a text is organised and held together: all those things that shape a text and make it coherent.

symbolise To use a symbol to represent something else, for example, black representing grief.

technique Another word for method. Writers use different techniques to create different **effects**.

theme A theme is a central idea in a text. Common themes in novels, films, poems and other literary texts include: loyalty, love, race, betrayal, poverty, good versus evil, and so on.

verb Word used to describe an action or state of being.

viewpoint A writer's or character's point of view: their attitudes, beliefs and opinions.

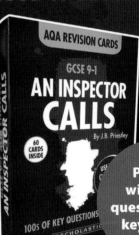
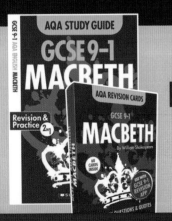